UN Security Council

This volume comprehensively evaluates the current state and future reform prospects of the UN Security Council and provides the most accessible and rigorous treatment of the subject of UN reform to date. Apart from a couple of critical eyes in the academic community, few have asked the pertinent questions that this volume seeks to address: Will the enlargement of the council constitute a reform? Could the inclusion of countries such as India, Germany, Japan, and Brazil markedly improve the council's agency?

In response, this book focuses on:

• the role and agency of the UN Security Council;
• the history of the reform debate;
• an expanded council;
• working method reforms;
• enhancing agency.

As the future of the UN Security Council continues to be the focus of fierce debate, this book will be essential reading for students of international relations, international organizations, and international security studies.

Peter Nadin is a researcher, policy analyst, and consultant based in Sydney, Australia. His research interests include UN peace operations, armed groups, leadership in UN missions, and the UN Security Council. He has previously worked as a project associate at United Nations University in Tokyo.

Global Institutions

Edited by Thomas G. Weiss
The CUNY Graduate Center, New York, USA
and Rorden Wilkinson
University of Sussex, Brighton, UK

About the series

The "Global Institutions Series" provides cutting-edge books about many aspects of what we know as "global governance." It emerges from our shared frustrations with the state of available knowledge—electronic and print-wise, for research and teaching—in the area. The series is designed as a resource for those interested in exploring issues of international organization and global governance. And since the first volumes appeared in 2005, we have taken significant strides toward filling conceptual gaps.

The series consists of three related "streams" distinguished by their blue, red, and green covers. The blue volumes, comprising the majority of the books in the series, provide user-friendly and short (usually no more than 50,000 words) but authoritative guides to major global and regional organizations, as well as key issues in the global governance of security, the environment, human rights, poverty, and humanitarian action among others. The books with red covers are designed to present original research and serve as extended and more specialized treatments of issues pertinent for advancing understanding about global governance. And the volumes with green covers—the most recent departure in the series—are comprehensive and accessible accounts of the major theoretical approaches to global governance and international organization.

The books in each of the streams are written by experts in the field, ranging from the most senior and respected authors to first-rate scholars at the beginning of their careers. In combination, the three components of the series—blue, red, and green—serve as key resources for faculty, students, and practitioners alike. The works in the blue and green streams have value as core and complementary readings in courses on, among other things, international organization, global governance, international law, international relations, and international political economy; the red volumes allow further reflection and investigation in these and related areas.

The books in the series also provide a segue to the foundation volume that offers the most comprehensive textbook treatment available dealing with all the major issues, approaches, institutions, and actors in contemporary global governance—our edited work *International Organization and Global Governance* (2014)—a volume to which many of the authors in the series have contributed essays.

Understanding global governance—past, present, and future—is far from a finished journey. The books in this series nonetheless represent significant steps toward a better way of conceiving contemporary problems and issues as well as, hopefully, doing something to improve world order. We value the feedback from our readers and their role in helping shape the on-going development of the series.

A complete list of titles appears at the end of this book. The most recent titles in the series are:

International Organizations and Military Affairs (2016)
by Hyllke Dijkstra

The International Committee of the Red Cross (2nd edition, 2016)
by David P. Forsythe and Barbara Ann J. Rieffer-Flanagan

The Arctic Council (2016)
by Douglas C. Nord

Human Development and Global Institutions (2016)
by Richard Ponzio and Arunabha Ghosh

NGOs and Global Trade (2016)
by Erin Hannah

Brazil as a Rising Power (2016)
edited by Kai Michael Kenkel and Philip Cunliffe

The United Nations as a Knowledge System (2015)
by Nanette Archer Svenson

UN Security Council Reform

Peter Nadin

Routledge
Taylor & Francis Group

LONDON AND NEW YORK

First published 2016 by Routledge

2 Park Square, Milton Park, Abingdon, Oxfordshire OX14 4RN
711 Third Avenue, New York, NY 10017

Routledge is an imprint of the Taylor & Francis Group, an informa business

First issued in paperback 2017

British Library Cataloguing in Publication Data
A catalogue record for this book is available from the British Library

Library of Congress Cataloging in Publication Data
A catalog record for this book has been requested

ISBN: 978-1-138-92022-4 (hbk)
ISBN: 978-1-138-47766-7 (pbk)

Typeset in Times New Roman
by Taylor & Francis Books

Contents

List of tables

Acknowledgement

First and foremost, I would like to thank Thomas Weiss, Rorden Wilkinson, and Nick Micinski for their support throughout the process. I would also like to extend my thanks to Nicola Parkin, Lydia de Cruz, Paola Celli, and Cinqué Hicks. Their assistance has been invaluable.

As this book draws on my doctoral thesis, I wish to also thank my supervisors Drew Cottle, Emilian Kavalski, and David Walton. They engaged with my work, corrected countless drafts, and cared for me throughout—their guidance has been invaluable. They are each formative figures in my life and I greatly appreciate their tutorage.

I must also extend a word of thanks to the people I have met while researching this volume. To those interviewees who gave so generously of their time and provided such useful insight, thank you.

Finally, I would like to thank my partner Mariko, as well as my family and friends for their love and unyielding encouragement. I would especially like to thank my mother and father for impressing upon me the importance of education. I hope I use this gift to make a difference in the world.

Acronyms and Abbreviations

DPA	Department of Political Affairs
DPKO	Department of Peacekeeping Operations
ICTFY	International Criminal Tribunal for the Former Yugoslavia
ICTR	International Criminal Tribunal for Rwanda
MINUGUA	United Nations Verification Mission in Guatemala
MINURCAT	United Nations Mission in the Central African Republic and Chad
MINUSCA	United Nations Multidimensional Integrated Stabilisation Mission in the Central Africa Republic
MINUSMA	United Nations Multidimensional Integrated Stabilisation Mission in Mali
MONUC	United Nations Organisation in the Democratic Republic of the Congo
MONUSCO	United Nations Organisation Stabilisation Mission in the Democratic Republic of the Congo
PBC	Peacebuilding Commission
SRSG	Special Representative of the Secretary-General
UNAMET	United Nations Assistance Mission in East Timor
UNAMID	United Nations–African Union Mission in Darfur
UNAMIR	United Nations Assistance Mission in Rwanda
UNAMSIL	United Nations Mission in Sierra Leone
UNEF I	United Nations Emergency Force I
UNITAF	United Task Force (Somalia)
UNMISS	United Nations Mission in South Sudan
UNOSOM I/II/II	United Nations Operation in Somalia (I/II/III)
UNPREDP	United Nations Preventive Deployment Force
UNPROFOR	United Nations Protection Force
UNTAES	United Nations Transitional Administration for Eastern Slavonia, Baranja and Western Sirmium

UNTAET   United Nations Transitional Administration in
             East Timor
SPM   Special Political Mission

List of Other Acronyms and Abbreviations

ACT   Accountability Coherence and Transparency
AU   African Union
C-10   Committee of Ten (African common position)
CAR   The Central African Republic
CARICOM   Caribbean Community
DRC   Democratic Republic of the Congo
E-10   The 10 Elected members of the UN Security Council
ECOWAS   Economic Community of West African States
EEG   Eastern European Group
G4   Group of Four (Japan, Germany, Brazil, and India)
GoS   Government of Sudan
GRULAC   Latin American and the Caribbean Group
ICISS   International Commission on Intervention and State
             Sovereignty
L-69   Cross-regional group of developing states on Security
             Council reform
MNF   Multinational Force
NAM   Non-Aligned Movement
P-5   The Permanent Five (China, France, Russia, the United
             Kingdom and the United States)
PoC   Protection of Civilians
RNtoV   Responsibility not to veto
RtoP   Responsibility to Protect
SIS/ASIS   Small Island States/Association of Small Island States
UfC   Uniting for Consensus
WEOG   Western Europe and Others Group

Introduction

- **Structure of the volume**
- **Questions that require an answer**

The anchor of faith, the growing wheat of hope, and the heart of charity adorn the walls of the United Nations Security Council Chamber in New York City. In the center of the chamber hangs a mural, which depicts a phoenix rising from the ashes of the Second World War. Surrounding the image of the phoenix are scenes of hope for a new world devoid of conflict and human suffering. It is clear that both Arnstein Arneberg and Per Krohg sought to encapsulate, through the interiors, the expectations held for the council.[1] Lofty expectations are, however, seldom met. For the council this adage could not hold more truth. The council was expected to operate as the custodian of international order in the postwar era. As the preeminent international institution, the council, through its decisions, mandated operations, and enforcement actions directly influences the present and the future state of international peace and security. Throughout its history, the council has proven a remarkably adaptable and enduring citadel at the center of international politics; and continues to stand as the "most powerful international institution in the history of the nation-state system."[2]

Yet, contorted by structural power politics, the council has often been unable to suppress the various threats to international peace and security that have beset the world. This has led many critics to bemoan the council for its failure to "act swiftly and effectively to contain international crises."[3] The failures of Rwanda, Somalia, and Bosnia continue to loom large, while a host of new crises have come to confound the council and stretch the credibility of international interventionism. More recently, the council has dropped the ball on Darfur, Sri Lanka, and Syria.

The panacea for the would-be reformers is a radical transformation of the council—reforming the composition of the council and the ways

Introduction

it works. Stephen M. Walt explains the predominant argument for reform:

> We all know why the United States, the United Kingdom, France, Russia, and China are permanent members with veto rights on the Security Council: The first four won World War II (well, France helped) and China has nearly a quarter of the world's population. But the present structure is one of the world's great anachronisms: Germany is now more important than either Britain or France and states such as India, Brazil, Japan, or South Africa (and some others) would be plausible contenders for permanent status too. Plenty of people – including former U.N. Secretary-General Kofi Annan – have tried to do something about this obvious absurdity, but efforts at reform are repeatedly stymied by a collective inability to agree on how the Security Council should be altered and by the P5's disinterest in diluting their own special status. But make no mistake: The present structure makes no sense.[4]

Critics of the status quo, like Walt, speak of the most glaring anachronism: a permanent cadre that includes the United Kingdom and France but excludes India, Germany, Brazil, and Japan. The would-be reformers claim that the long-term exclusion of these powers will negatively affect the legitimacy of the council. They argue that the council is not effective, because it is not reflective of the geopolitical realities of the twenty-first century. To secure the council's enduring legitimacy, the reformists have argued for the creation of a permanent 11 (P-11), which would be inclusive of the current P-5 and a selection of the great and emerging powers of Asia, Africa, Latin America, and Europe. The aspirants for the six new permanent seats include Japan and India (from the Asia-Pacific), Brazil (from Latin America), Germany (from Western Europe) and South Africa, Nigeria, Ethiopia, Algeria, and Egypt (from Africa). The aspirants have warned that if the status quo remains and system is not altered in favor of so-called twenty-first century realities, the disenfranchised countries of the global south will abandon the United Nations (UN) peace and security system in a favor of other constellations, organizations, and alliance structures. This line of argument will be referred to as new permanency.

Both the principled and the covetous view new permanency as a threat. The prospect of new permanent members has stirred a hornet's nest of neighborhood rivalries: Brazil and Argentina, India and Pakistan, Italy and Germany, China and Japan, and between the big five in Africa. The principled, on the other hand, harbor "concerns about how council members for life could ever be held accountable."[5] These disaffected voices have put a counter-proposal. They envisage an enlarged council, but one without any new permanent seats. On this side of the debate, the would-be reformists believe that the council would be better served through the creation of a third category of membership—renewable seats. This line of argument will be referred to as renewability. A third group of reformists have opted for a different track, devoting themselves instead to the question of working methods—the procedures and mechanics of council decision-making. The working methods reformists have worked from within and without to change the way the council works day-to-day. Interestingly, those reformists working from a seat at the horseshoe table have proven more successful. Since the council's renaissance in the early 1990s many innovative practices have been introduced and many more slated. The battle of working methods reform has been one of sustaining innovative practices and safeguarding them against distortion, while exploring new ones.[6]

Overall, the membership has remained highly fragmented on the issue of reform, and as such no single group or coalition "has come close to the support needed to amend the UN Charter."[7] Currently, debate is trapped in the perpetual merry-go-round of Intergovernmental Negotiations on Security Council Reform (IGN). In session, member-states fervently hold to their positions, regurgitate rhetoric, and utilize procedural maneuver to restrict debate. More than anything else, member-states, and the coalitions to which they belong, have come to be defined by their lack of capacity for compromise.

Structure of the volume

This book is divided into six chapters. The first offers a historical contextualization of the council's role in international politics. In doing so, this chapter will attempt answer two important questions: What is the council on paper? What is the council in practice? The second chapter offers an explanatory theory of how the council works. The theory will explain council agency (its capacity to act in the world) through a discussion of the elements of legitimacy, alignment, solution, political will, resources, and leadership. As Edward Luck suggested in the preface to his book *UN Security Council: Practice and Promise*, "the only way to get a sense of where it [the council] is going is to begin with some understanding of where it started, what route it has taken, and how far it has come."[8] This chapter borrows the spirit of Luck's call.

Chapter three offers a summary of the current state of play in the ongoing and fractious reform debate. A profile of the key positions, coalitions (C-10, G4, Uniting for Consensus, and L-69), and countries (Japan, Germany, India, Brazil, South Africa, Nigeria, Ethiopia, Egypt, and Algeria) will be offered. In addition, the meandering narrative of the reform stalemate will be retold. Chapter four seeks to scrutinize the claims that underpin the argument for expansion. The claims of would-be reformists will be critiqued. A series of weigh stations will be constructed, and then used to check the extraordinary claims presented by the promoters of both the new permanency and renewability arguments: legitimacy; twenty-first century geopolitical realities; power projection; democratization and inclusion; efficiency; "lowest common denominator-ism;"[9] and contribution to the maintenance of international peace and security.

Chapter five explores the working methods reforms. Slated, stillborn, and embryonic reforms will be placed under the microscope, and a series of questions posed: What is the internal logic of the method? And would its introduction improve the agency of the council? Chapter six offers a series of recommendatory thoughts, which flow naturally from the preceding chapters. The recommendations found in this chapter are intended to encourage policy-makers and decision-makers to think afresh about reform. The chapter contains a suggested model for compromise, as well as a collection of musings on the questions of strategy, evaluation, the interactivity of meetings, sanctions, and peace operations.

Questions that require an answer

This volume seeks to subject the claims of would-be reformists to sustained scrutiny by posing a series of questions, in sequence. Firstly, what is reform? This would seem to be an obvious and fundamental first question, but it is a question that is easily cast aside in the heat of debate, where the pursuit of individual status overrides collectivist concerns vis-à-vis performance. This volume calls for a re-orientation of the debate. Reform is about the changing something for the better. Hence, the debate on reform should be seeking to answer Edward Luck's question: "Which reform steps would lead to better performance, not just improved process?"[10] This volume contends that the fundamental problem with the reform debate is that it is focused disproportionately on questions of membership over questions of mechanics. Too much attention is paid to questions of composition, while too little attention is paid to how members might improve their interactions and make better decisions in the interests of peace and security.

Secondly, would the inclusion of countries such as India, Germany, Japan, Brazil, South Africa, and Nigeria markedly improve the council's capacity to act in the world? Does giving the powerful a seat at the table make the council a more powerful body? Is such a plan future proof (i.e. adaptable to future power shifts)? The aspirants continue to expound the virtue of their position though the invocation of terms such as democratization, representativeness, accountability, and equity. Yet, the play for permanency also exhibits all the hallmarks of a self-interested power grab, which begs the question: would adding a host of permanent members serve to undermine representativeness and accountability by reinforcing privilege?

Thirdly, is enlargement actually a reform? An enlarged council would not necessary be an effective one. If expanded, the council would inevitably sacrifice a degree of efficiency. The more significant question, however, is the potential for reforms to induce indecision. A new cadre of permanent members may well further polarize debate on contentious issues. Is it appropriate for an executive organ to expand until it becomes unwieldy and indecisive?

Notes

1 The government of Norway donated the chamber to the UN. Arnstein Arneberg was the architect and Per Krohg was the artist of the mural.
2 Ian Hurd and Bruce Cronin, "Introduction," in *The UN Security Council and the Politics of International Authority*, eds. Ian Hurd and Bruce Cronin (Abingdon: Routledge, 2008), 3.
3 Reuters, "El Baradei Criticises Security Council," *Al Jazeera*, 26 March 2006. http://www.aljazeera.com/archive/2006/03/200849125843772160.html.
4 Stephen M. Walt, "The UN Security Council. What's Up with That?," *Foreign Policy*. 7 April 2015: para. 6. http://foreignpolicy.com/2015/04/07/the-u-n-security-council-whats-up-with-that/.
5 Edward C. Luck, *The UN Security Council: Practice and Promise* (Abingdon: Routledge, 2006), 119.
6 Thomas G. Weiss and Karen E. Young, "Compromise and Credibility: Security Council Reform?" *Security Dialogue* 36, no. 2 (2005): 131–154.
7 Stewart Patrick and Kara McDonald, *UN Security Council Enlargement and US Interests* (New York: Council on Foreign Relations, 2010), 3.
8 Luck, *The UN Security Council*, xvii.
9 Anonymous Interviewee, Interview with Author, June 2011.
10 Luck, *The UN Security Council*, 125.

1   The UN Security Council

- **From the League of Nations to the United Nations: evolution not revolution**
- **What is the UN Security Council (on paper)?**
- **What is the UN Security Council (in practice)?**
- **Conclusion**

Rising like a phoenix from the ashes of the Second World War and the wreckage of the League of Nations, the UN was given a broad-reaching set of responsibility—"to maintain international peace and security, facilitate the development of friendly relations among nations, promote social progress, better living standards and human rights."[1] Of the broad-ranging tasks given to the organization, the UN Security Council was charged with arguably the most important—"primary responsibility for the maintenance of international peace and security."[2] Over the course of the last seventy years the council has proven a remarkably resilient and adaptable piece of international machinery.

The overarching aim of this chapter is to set the context for the volume, and begin the process of understanding "where it [the council] started, what route it has taken, and how far it has come."[3] To address this aim, the chapter will provide an overview of the history of the council, as a study of philosophical and historical debates that underpinned the League of Nations and the UN is instructive in the context of the contemporary council.

From the League of Nations to the United Nations: evolution not revolution

As far back as the eighteenth century, states had met, on several occasions, to forge, what Kant referred to as "a federation of free states," "a league of nations," "a compact among nations," and "a league of peace (foedus pacificum),"[4] a diplomatic forum for avoiding global conflicts. The first attempt was the Concert of Europe, founded at the Congress of Vienna in 1815. The second attempt was the League of Nations, founded at the signing of the Treaty of Versailles in 1919. The third was the UN, founded at San Francisco in 1945. Each was designed to overcome the defects of its predecessor.

The delegates at Dumbarton Oaks were fully aware of the failures of the global order that had preceded the war (WWII). The failure of the League of Nations has been attributed to "its lack of power, lack of universality, lack of solidarity (or cooperation) between members, and the exaggerated equality between the great and small powers, caused by the increase in the number of non-permanent members on the [league's executive] Council."[5] The Council of the League of Nations also met infrequently and was notoriously slow to respond in times of crisis.[6] It was an organization infused with a spirit of consensualism, where compliance was an option, sanctions not compulsory, and the Covenant ambiguous regarding the authorization of the use of force. The UN was intended to represent a reformed wider and permanent system of general security. Not so much a revolution, but an evolution.

The first step was made on 14 August 1941, when US President Franklin Delano Roosevelt (FDR), and Prime Minister of United Kingdom Winston Churchill signed the Atlantic Charter. The charter contained a "vague and tentative commitment to some sort of international organization that would promote peace by the establishment of a wider and permanent system of general security."[7] A further 24 nations, including the other major allied powers (the Union of Soviet Socialist Republic [USSR] and the Republic of China), pledged to uphold the principles of the Declaration of the United Nations.[8] Following the signing of the Atlantic Treaty, the concept of the UN began to ferment in the offices of the State Department in Washington and at the Commonwealth and Foreign Office in London. Roosevelt and Churchill also began to talk of a postwar world. The US President recognized the deficiencies of the League system, and in response proposed the four-policemen model.[9] Under this model, the United States, the UK, the USSR and China would act in concert to provide security through force of power. The four policemen were to be the trustees of the postwar order.[10]

These nascent ideas and others were taken to three conferences on the creation of an international peace and security organization—the first at Dumbarton Oaks, the second at Yalta, and the third at San Francisco. Arguably the most important of these conferences was the Washington conversations on the creation of an international peace and security organization held at Dumbarton Oaks in 1944. At Dumbarton Oaks, discussion focused on the creation of a council that would have the power and authority necessary to maintain international peace and security. This council was to become known as the Security Council. Over the course of a couple of weeks, the delegates discussed the composition of the council and its membership, size, meetings, powers, functions, and procedures.[11]

Each delegation brought differing proposals to the table, and at each juncture, compromise was achieved, except on the matter of the veto, which was deferred to the leaders' summit at Yalta. At Yalta, the big three approved a voting formula that allowed the permanent members of the council to exercise a veto on substantive decisions, but not on procedural matters. The Dumbarton Oaks drafts (officially entitled Proposals for the Establishment of a General International Organization) and the so-called Yalta formula were then taken to San Francisco for the United Nations Conference on International Organization. At San Francisco, delegates from 46 nations assembled to draft the Charter of the United Nations.

Notably, the proposals regarding the council passed the convention at San Francisco without significant amendment. This is not to say that the proposals themselves were not controversial. The procedural and deliberative processes of the conference allowed the smaller nations to voice their concerns; and the smaller nations had one concern in particular—the veto.

Australian Foreign Minister Herbert Vere Evatt was the vocal leader of the anti-veto lobby. Evatt and his supporters posed 23 questions relating the use of the veto and issued over a dozen amendments.[12] In the end, no substantive changes were made at San Francisco. The smaller nations accepted the ultimatum—without the veto there would be no UN. The conference, however, had served the purpose of legitimizing the inequalities inherent to the system.[13]

What is the UN Security Council (on paper)?

Chapters V, VI, VII and VIII of the Charter of the UN lay down the fundamental principles of the Security Council in what might be described as a constitution of sorts. Chapter V sets out the council's composition, voting rules, procedures, functions and powers. Chapter VI entitled the Pacific Settlement of Disputes, calls upon member states to utilize alternative dispute resolution methods in cases where a dispute might likely escalate to open war. Chapter VII, entitled Action with Respect to Threats to the Peace, Breaches of the Peace, and Acts of Aggression, provides the council with the power to determine the existence of a threat to international peace and security and the power to act upon any threat by way of either non-military (sanctions) or military means (use of force). The final, less cited, chapter of the charter, which pertains to the Security Council, is Chapter VIII—Regional Arrangements. This chapter sets the ground rules for UN interaction with regional organizations, and states clearly that only the Security Council possesses the right to authorize enforcement action.[14]

It would now be prudent to examine these sections in a little more detail, starting with Chapter V. This chapter begins by outlining the composition of the council. Article 23 (1) states that the council shall consist of 15 members of the UN. Originally the council consisted of 11 members. In 1966, the council was expanded to 15. The issue of size was a question raised at Dumbarton Oaks. A balance was struck and the big three decided on the number 11. Not all of these fifteen members are considered equal, however. Although Article 1 affirms sovereign equality, for the council this principle does not apply. Article 23 (1) and (2) distinguish between a permanent five (or P-5) and non-permanent 10 (or E-10).[15] The P-5 include the United States, the UK, France, the Republic of China (ROC) and the USSR.[16]

The United States, the UK, and the USSR were the undisputed great powers of the era and the victors of the Second World War. The ROC and France were chosen for a variety of reasons. The charter legitimately enshrines P-5 dominance over the council. This dominance takes the form of a veto. Although coded in rather "nifty language,"[17] the veto is found in Article 27 (3):

> Decisions of the Security Council on all other matters shall be made by an affirmative vote of nine members including the concurring votes of the permanent members.[18]

The veto is an effective safeguard on the interests of the five; used to protect their own interests or the interests of an ally or proxy.[19] Although, the veto can elicit paralysis, it also serves as a concert function—a term coined by David Bosco.[20] One the inherent problems with the League of Nations was that, as an international organization, it failed to maintain continuity of permanent membership. The League council was a veritable revolving door, with permanent members withdrawing from the organization whenever their actions were condemned. Instituting a veto was one way of insuring the participation of all the great powers. When they (the P-5) all agree (or can tolerate a proposal), action can be taken. When they disagree, action can be blocked. The veto is a safety valve, a flag that signals to tread carefully. The veto also forces the P-5 to negotiate daily and "compromise on contentious issues,"[21] which builds a degree of cohesion and under-standing between them. In all, the veto has been used on a total of 271 occasions (as of 1 October 2015) to block council action, and has been threatened on countless other occasions. The veto attracts a great deal of media attention when it is exercised, and rightly so. Yet most coun-cil business is conducted without reference to the veto. In fact, in the post–Cold War era, it has been used sparingly by the three major powers—United States (16 times), China (8 times), and Russia (12 times). Since 23 December 1989, the veto has been exercised on 30 occasions, an average just over one a year (Appendix I).

It was FDR's vision that "might be placed at the disposal of right."[22] For him and the other leaders this equation could only be answered by the institutionalization of the four-policemen concept. The idea being that these policemen would act as the providers of security, while the other members of the organization would be the con-sumers of security. As bearers of the burden of this responsibility, the P-5 expected to be given the ability to operate the council as their domain. The institutionalized privilege of the veto provides the P-5 with that ability. The founders knew that one of the primary weaknesses of the League was its lack of so-called teeth. The failings of the League were not to be replicated—the council would be given the power of enfor-cement. An international armed force, placed at the disposal of the UN, would provide the requisite military might. Churchill later (in March 1946) spoke of how a UN armed force might operate:

> The United Nations Organisation must immediately begin to be equipped with an international armed force. In such a matter we can only go step by step, but we must begin now. I propose that each of the Powers and States should be invited to delegate a cer-tain number of air squadrons to the service of the world organisa-tion. These squadrons would be trained and prepared in their own countries, but would move around in rotation from one country to another. They would wear the uniform of their own countries but with different badges.[23]

Churchill talked about equipping the UN with a military backbone so that it could speedily enforce its decisions whenever it "arrived at a judgment based on international law."[24] An international armed force would carry out the enforcement of resolutions. Air power would be centerpiece of such a force.[25] Command and control of these forces would be managed by a Military Staff Committee (MSC),[26] as an extension of the Combined Chiefs of Staff system that had operated in Europe during the Second World War.[27] The committee would consist of military representatives of the P-5, plus other major states, to be included on the basis of contribution.

Force, however, was to be used only as a last resort. The council possessed a range of options. It could first resort to the use of other instruments, notably sanctions. Chapter VII of the charter sets out a very clear logical progression or escalation in a possible council response. The first step in this progression is Article 40, which refers to provisional measures—taken in order to not enflame a situation. If compliance was not forthcoming, however, Article 41 could be "employed to give effect" to the decisions of the council. Article 41 contains a detailed list of possible sanctions which might be imposed in order to elicit compliance. If sanctions proved inadequate, step three, the final stage along the line of escalation could be invoked—Article 42—use of force.

A similar staged progression was outlined in Chapter VI of the charter, concerning the peaceful settlement of political and diplomatic disputes—those being, disputes that have not escalated to the stage of open violent interstate conflict. At Dumbarton Oaks, much discussion was had on the topic of exactly how much authority would be granted to the council in respect to these types of disputes. In the end, an atmosphere of recommendation rather than imposition predominated the text. If a dispute arose between two or more parties, it was incumbent upon the parties to seek a solution through a range of peaceful means (including arbitration, mediation, negotiation, enquiry, conciliation, judicial settlement or a resort to regional agencies or arrangements).[28] At this stage of the process the council could call upon the parties to settle their dispute peacefully[29] or recommend processes or methods of adjustment.[30] Nevertheless, if the dispute persisted, in spite of the parties' best efforts, the dispute would be referred to the council for a recommendation on the terms of settlement.[31]

The council communicates its decisions (under Chapter VII) and its recommendations (under Chapter VI) through a formal text—known as a resolution. Although the charter does not make clear a structural separation between Chapter VI and VII, in practice, Chapter VII resolutions are considered to be binding, while Chapter VI resolutions are not. Erika De Wet explains the difference in her book, *The Chapter VII Powers of the United Nations Security Council*:

> The whole aim of separating these chapters is to distinguish between voluntary and binding measures. Whereas the pacific

settlement of disputes provided by the former is underpinned by the consent of the parties, binding measures in terms of Chapter VII are characterised by the absence of such consent.[32]

Every resolution begins with the reasoning behind its adoption. These stanzas are known as the perambulatory clauses. Following the preamble are the operative clauses. These clauses express in words what the council has decided or recommended—i.e. the council's decided course of action on the matter. The council can also communicate through the use of presidential statements. These statements are shorter than resolutions, usually only two pages in length, and adopted by consensus and signed by the President of the Council. Presidential statements are not legally binding and are generally used to convey support or augment resolutions.[33] The membership of the UN is of the understanding that the council adopts resolutions and presidential statements on their behalf, as stated in Article 24 (1). Furthermore, members understand that they are obligated, not only to accept the resolutions of the council, but to carry them into effect. The effectiveness (as a product of legitimacy) of the council depends on this provision being upheld.

In carrying out its functions, and adopting resolutions under both Chapter VI and VII, the council operates with considerable flexibility and discretionary power. The charter gives the council this power in order that it might "get things done."[34] Flexibility is made available in the areas procedure (Article 30),[35] meeting locations,[36] the credentials of the representatives at the table,[37] the establishment of subsidiary bodies (Article 29), and the inclusion of non-members in the meetings of the council.[38] Far and away the most important discretionary power is the provision to define threats to international peace and security (contained in Article 39):

> The Security Council shall determine the existence of any threat to the peace, breach of the peace, or act of aggression and shall make recommendations, or decide what measures shall be taken in accordance with Articles 41 and 42, to maintain or restore international peace and security.[39]

If the council determines a situation constitutes a threat to international peace and security, that situation is a threat, by definition. The council's scope is theoretically unlimited; this point was made clear to an Australian delegate after he questioned the council's authority in relation to the creation of a UN protectorate in the Free State of

Trieste. A US diplomat rebuffed his question with the following answer: "Any spot on the surface of the Earth where for whatever reason, conflicts may break out and men may be at each other's throats is a spot of legitimate concern to the Security Council."[40]

The US diplomat was completely correct, the council could involve itself anywhere, at any time, but only if its permanent members consented. Over the course of the last 70 years, the council has come to interpret the charter in variety of innovative ways. The council uses the spirit of certain articles and chapters, rather than their prescriptive processes. If the Council agrees on the imposition of targeted sanctions, the council will invoke Article 41. On the other hand, if the council agrees on binding measures or the authorization of the use of force, under certain conditions by one of its peacekeeping operations, the council will invoke Chapter VII. The council as envisaged on paper is very different to the Council in practice. The next section briefly charts the course of its history through phases of improvisation, innovation and hyperactivity.

What is the UN Security Council (in practice)?

The Security Council envisaged by the founders of the United Nations does not exist, and never did, except on paper. Many of the provisions of the charter were never enacted and many of the council's functions passed away when the paralysis of the Cold War set in. The Security Council, as a reflection of the international political landscape, was for the most part under-utilized throughout the Cold War. But that is not to say that the council lost all utility. During the Cold War era, the council learned to improvise and innovate. It dealt with the questions of Spain, Greece, Iran, Indonesia, India-Pakistan, before taking on the now obdurate Palestinian question, the Suez Crisis, the Congo, Cyprus, and later Southwestern Africa and the problems (Namibia, Angola, Southern Rhodesia, Zambia, and South Africa) emanating principally from the apartheid regime in South Africa. In addressing these questions the council employed the use of military observers and later interpositional peacekeepers, as well as commissions of investigation. The council even went as far as to establish an international protectorate known as the Free Territory of Trieste[41] and a UN state-building force in the Congo.[42]

The imagined processes of response were done away with, out of sheer practicality, and the council began to work very differently from what was imagined by the founders. The largest gap between Charter and practice concerned the use of force. With the arrival of the Cold War, Articles 43–47, covering UN control of military enforcement activities, became dead letters. Instead the Council established itself as the sole licenser of the use of force. The licensees (commonly referred to as coalitions of the willing) were collections of member-states directing the use of military force and carrying out the terms of the council licenses (trigger or authorizing resolutions). The council first licensed the use of force in 1950 "to repel the armed attack [by North Korea] and to restore international peace and security to the area."[43] Council authorization of full-scale military enforcement did not gain currency following the Korean War, however.[44] Aside from, and instead of, military enforcement, which was seen to have limited utility, the council, in dealing with conflicts, came to place its hopes in the invention of peacekeeping.

UN peacekeeping, in its traditional sense, emerged in 1956 during the Suez Crisis. With the council deadlocked following UK and French vetoes, the matter was taken to the General Assembly under the Uniting for Peace resolution. During the emergency session, Canadian Secretary of State for External Affairs Lester B. Pearson recognized that a ceasefire and withdrawal were not enough and proposed the establishment of an international force to police the ceasefire line—Israeli forces on one side and the Egyptians on the other. The General Assembly endorsed Pearson's idea,[45] and charged the Secretary-General Dag Hammarskjöld with hastily developing a guiding doctrine for the interpositional force—to be known as the United Nations Emergency Force (UNEF I). The UN had crafted for itself a new conflict management instrument in peacekeeping, enacted through improvisational maneuver. Following UNEF, the Security Council authorized a further 13 peacekeeping operations before the end of the Cold War. The most interesting and radical of these was the United Nations Operation in the Congo (ONUC). The operation was considered a pyrrhic victory for the UN. However, it presented the most remarkable picture of future peacekeeping.

The UN would have to wait some time before a thaw in relations was to be realized. The international political landscape did begin to shift towards the end of the 1980s.[46] The council too began to reflect this relative shift in mood. The end of the Cold War heralded the so-called New World Order, brought forward in a spirit of renewed great power cooperation. When a council based solution took effect to end the Iran-Iraq War in 1986–1987, the council was said to have been unlocked. The adoption of resolution 678, which authorized the use of force (Gulf War) against Iraq in November 1990, was perhaps the more important and strongest exemplar of an unlocked council.[47] At the start of 1990, the council had passed a total of 646 resolutions; since then, the council has passed over 1500 resolutions. These resolutions have been concerned with such questions as Iran-Iraq, Afghanistan, Mozambique, Namibia, Central America and El Salvador, Somalia, the former Yugoslavia, Rwanda, Sierra Leone, the Democratic Republic of Congo, East Timor, Kosovo, the protection of civilians in armed conflict, international terrorism, and the proliferation of weapons of mass destruction (principally nuclear) in Iraq, Iran, and North Korea.

The council's activities in relation to these cases can be placed into five distinct categories—(1) normative and crosscutting; (2) quasi-legislative; (3) prevention of Chemical, Biological, Radiological, or Nuclear (CBRN) weapons proliferation; (4) international conflict; and (5) intrastate conflict. Excluding normative and crosscutting items, the Security Council has dealt with approximately 50 subjects over the course of the last 25 years (1990–present). The council's authority and the scope of its activities have expanded greatly. Over this time, the vast majority of the council's activities have been undertaken in relation to civil war. With the end of the Cold War, the incidence of intrastate war spiked, while the international conflicts to which the council was designed and accustomed to dealing with noticeably declined. Enabled by an emerging normative environment in international society, the council sought to expand its focus into areas of internal violence.[48] The effectiveness of the council in these situations is contingent on the council's ability to craft, chiefly through the use of peacekeeping, an effective and legitimate state. The little dirty wars of the 90s were particularly traumatic and complex, however. The previously under-utilized council was now dealing with multiple situations across four continents.

The Council dispatched a series of assistance missions to El Salvador, Namibia, Mozambique, and a more ambitious transitional administration mission to Cambodia. Emboldened by the positive outcomes, member-states, grew ever more ambitious. They soon deployed large numbers of peacekeepers to Somalia and the former Yugoslavia to assist in the delivery of humanitarian aid. The conceptual ground on which these missions were based was flawed, and both operations were ultimately ineffective. The sudden retrenchment in UN peacekeeping following the precipitate withdrawal of United Nations Operation in Somalia II (UNOSOM II) resulted, in part, to the collapse of the United Nations Assistance Mission in Rwanda (UNAMIR). The failure of the Security Council to halt the genocide in Rwanda is surely its supreme failure.

By contrast, the council has only involved itself in seven situations of interstate and regional conflict since the end of the Cold War—Iran-Iraq, Iraq-Kuwait, Armenia-Azerbaijan, Aouzou Strip (Libya-Chad), Great Lakes Region, Ethiopia-Eritrea, and Israel-Lebanon. Traditional interpositional peacekeeping was the instrument of choice in these situations, verifying agreed upon lines of demarcation. In many cases, the conflicts were simply frozen in time, rather than resolved.

Since 1991, the Security Council has also developed a capacity in the area of the proliferation of CBRN weapons. Three countries have been singled out for special attention—Iraq, its neighbor Iran, and North Korea. The effectiveness of the council, in its non-proliferation role, is determined by the council's ability to contain and then dismantle a target state's weapons program. In the case of Iraq (2001–2003), in spite of the Iraq disarmament saga of 2002–2003, the Security Council effectively disarmed Iraq.[49] In the case of Iran, the council's work has positively reinforced the efforts of the P-5+1 negotiations. North Korea, however, still continues to flout council demands.[50]

Finally, the council has undertaken work on the normative front, passing resolutions on the protection of civilians in armed conflict, women peace and conflict and children and armed conflict.[51] Since the terrorist attacks on 11 September 2001, the council has acted in a quasi-legislative matter. Resolutions 1373 and 1540 on terrorism and weapons of mass destruction compelled member states to adopt changes to their domestic law as legislated by the council.[52] Resolution 1373 authorized under Chapter VII, requires member-states to ratify existing international conventions on terrorism. In 2004, a similar resolution was adopted requiring member-states to regulate against the proliferation of weapons of mass destruction to prevent such weapons being acquired by non-state actors.[53]

With expanded scope, the council innovated—developing a new range of instruments, while fine-tuning already existing ones. These advancements in practice were clarified using a typology given impetus by the work of Secretaries-General Boutros Boutros-Ghali and Kofi Annan (an *Agenda for Peace* and its supplement; and *In Larger Freedom*).[54] Another dramatic development was in the area of international criminal law. The mass crimes inflicted on civilians in Rwanda and the former Yugoslavia could not go unpunished. In the name of justice and with the sense of guilt, the council established two tribunals— International Criminal Tribunal for Rwanda (ICTR) and the International Criminal Tribunal for the Former Yugoslavia (ICTFY)—covering the crimes committed in both countries.

Conclusion

The council's primary responsibility is the maintenance of international peace and security. The founders saw a council dealing with state-on-state crises, acts of aggression, and international conflict. The charter is evidence of this impression. It reads like a playbook on dealing with international disputes and conflict. Today, of the 78 items of which the council actively seized, only a handful can be characterized as a predominately state-on-state issue. The drafters, nevertheless, afforded their diplomatic successors the flexibility to constantly redefine the council's remit, and this is the essence of its enduring utility.

Notes

1 UN Department of Public Information, *The United Nations Today* (New York: UN Department of Public Information, 2008).
2 UN Charter, Chapter V, Article 24 (1).
3 Edward C. Luck, *UN Security Council: Practice and Promise* (Abingdon: Routledge, 2006), xvii.
4 Immanuel Kant, *Perpetual Peace: A Philosophical Sketch* (Minneapolis, Minn.: Filiquarian Publishing LLC, 2007), pp. 16–19
5 Russell S. Sobel, "The League of Nations Covenant and the United Nations Charter: An Analysis of Two Constitutions," *Constitutional Political Economy* 5, no. 2 (1994): 178.
6 The League only held 107 meetings in the space of nineteen years—an average of five meetings per year.
7 Warren F. Kimball, "The Atlantic Charter: With All Deliberate Speed," in *The Atlantic Charter,* eds. Douglas Brinkley and David R. Facey-Crowther (New York: St Martin's Press, 1994), 92.
8 The outcome document of the Arcadia Conference (January 1942).
9 Townsend Hoopes and Douglas Brinkley, *FDR and the Creation of the UN* (New Haven, Conn.: Yale University Press, 1997).
10 Stephen C. Schlesinger, *Act of Creation: The Founding of the United Nations* (Cambridge, Mass.: Basic Books, 2004).
11 Robert C. Hilderbrand, *Dumbarton Oaks: The Origins of the United Nations and the Search for Postwar Security* (Chapel Hill, N.C.: University of North Carolina Press, 2001).
12 Stephen Schlesinger, *Act of Creation: The Founding of the United Nations.*
13 Ian Hurd, *After Anarchy: Legitimacy and Power in the United Nations Security Council* (Princeton, N.J.: Princeton University Press, 2008).
14 UN Charter, Chapter VIII, Article 53 (1).
15 Many "non-permanent" countries and their representatives take offense to the use of the term, particularly when invoked by a permanent member. They prefer to be known as elected members of the council.
16 UN Charter, Chapter V, Article 23 (2). The Republic of China held the 'China' seat until 1972, when it was transferred to the PRC; the Soviet Union held a permanent seat until the dissolution of the Union in 1991, at this time the seat was transferred to the USSR's logical successor, the Russian Federation.
17 Paul Kennedy, *The Parliament of Man: The United Nations and the Quest for World Government* (London: Penguin Books, 2006), 35.
18 UN Charter, Chapter V, Article 27 (3).

19 Using the veto on behalf of a proxy is what one former Permanent Representative has described as a "veto for rent."

20 David Bosco, *Five to Rule Them All: The UN Security Council and the Making of the Modern World* (New York: Oxford University Press, 2009).

21 Bosco, *Five to Rule Them All*, 5.

22 James Traub, *The Best Intentions: Kofi Annan and the UN in the Era of American World Power* (New York: Farrar Straus & Giroux, 2006), 4.

23 Traub, *The Best Intentions*, 4.

24 Traub, *The Best Intentions*, 4.

25 Air power was in vogue at the time the Charter was drafted, so much so, that it was stated by US Vice President Wallace that an international air force would be used to "bomb aggressor nations mercilessly until they laid down their arms." Hilderbrand, *Dumbarton Oaks*, 142.

26 UN Charter, Chapter VII, Articles 46 and 47.

27 The Military Staff Committee would also function as an advisory body to the Security Council on questions of a military nature and the regulation of armaments.

28 UN Charter, Chapter VI, Article 33 (1).

29 UN Charter, Chapter VI, Article 33 (2).

30 UN Charter, Chapter VI, Article 36 (1).

31 UN Charter, Chapter VI, Article 37 (2).

32 Erica De Wet, *The Chapter VII Powers of the United Nations Security Council* (Portland, Oreg.: Hart Publishing, 2004), 39.

33 They are not particularly weighty and will not be regularly mentioned or analyzed as part of this thesis.

34 Paul Kennedy, *The Parliament of Man,* 35.

35 Article 30 allows the Council to adopt its own rules of procedure, however, the Council actually currently operates under provisional rules of procedure that were adopted in 1982.

36 UN Charter, Chapter V, Article 28 (3). The Council has met, on occasion, away from New York. The Council first met in London (Church House), and has since met in Paris and Addis Ababa.

37 UN Charter, Chapter V, Article 28 (2 and 3).

38 UN Charter, Chapter V, Article 31 and 32.

39 UN Charter, Chapter V, Article 39.

40 Bosco, *Five to Rule Them All*, 47.

41 Security Council resolution 16, 10 January 1947.

42 Security Council resolution 143, 17 July 1960.

43 Security Council resolution 84, 7 July 1950.

44 The United Nations Command (Korea) existed as a UN force in name only; the endeavor was essentially a US-led multinational operation supported by the British Commonwealth and Western Europe.

45 General Assembly resolution 998, 2 November 1956.

46 Thomas G. Weiss, David P. Forsythe, Richard A. Coate, and Kelly-Kate Pease, *The United Nations and Changing World Politics* (Boulder, Colo.: Westview Press, 2010), 35.

47 For the first time in forty years (Korean War), the UN Security Council authorized the use of force to repel an aggressor state.

48 As well as issues previously considered to lie in the area of domestic jurisdiction. Article 2 (7).

49 George Lopez and David Cortright, "Containing Iraq: Sanctions Worked," *Foreign Affairs* (July/August 2004).

50 In the non-proliferation space, the work of the Security Council exhibits a double standard: non-signatories to the nuclear non-proliferation treaty (NPT) India, Pakistan, and Israel all possess sizable nuclear arsenals, all of which have been developed without warranting the scrutiny of the Security Council.

51 *Normative and Cross-Cutting: Protection of Civilians in Armed Conflict* (res. 1265), *Women in Peace and Security* (res. 1325), *International Terrorism, Peace and Security in Africa* (res. 1170), *International Peace and Security, Children and Armed Conflict* (res. 1261), *AIDS and Peacekeeping* (res. 1308), *Peacekeeping* (res. 1327), *Strengthening Co-operation with Troop Contributing Countries* (res. 1353), *The Role of the Security Council in the Prevention of Armed Conflicts* (res. 1366), *Regional Organization Cooperation* (res. 1631), *Peacebuilding* (res. 1645).

52 Ian Johnstone, "Legislation and Adjudication in the UN Security Council: Bringing Down the Deliberative Deficit," *American Journal of International Law* 102, no. 2 (2008): 275–308.

53 Andrea Bianchi, "Assessing the Effectiveness of the UN Security Council's Anti-Terrorism Measures: The Quest for Legitimacy and Cohesion," *European Journal of International Law* 17, no. 5 (2007): 881–919.

54 Terms like peace enforcement and preventive diplomacy were introduced into the UN lexicon.

2 The agency of the UN Security Council

- **Legitimacy**
- **Mobilization**
- **Forming a response**
- **Implementation**
- **Conclusion**

The overarching aim of this chapter is to better understand how this enigmatic institution works. An explanatory model for council agency will be built and used to better understand the mechanics of the council. For the council, agency can be defined as its capacity to act in world. Members of the UN, generally, and the members of the council, specifically, give the council its agency. It is determined by a complex inter-action of forces: legitimacy, political will, permanent member alignment, leadership, resources, and the quality and content of its output. The model will attempt to trace the currents and eddies of typical council decision-making processes. By understanding what determines council agency, one can come to understand the council's defects and deficiencies. As reform is concerned with repairing defects and addressing capacity deficits, a discussion of agency seems an obvious place to begin. In short, the following is a description of the workflow of council's ad-hoc and semi-institutionalized processes for managing international crises.

Legitimacy

With the risk of beginning this chapter rather abruptly, it should be recognized, from the outset, that legitimacy is the basic condition for council agency. Without it the council would cease to hold authority into international politics. Legitimacy is defined as "the degree to which the UN membership recognizes the council as having both the right and the competence to act on behalf of the international community in addressing issues related to international peace and security."[1] Upon affixing their names to the charter, member-states recognize that the council has the "right and the competence to make binding decisions for the rest of the community."[2] ｟why｠

By contrast, the kernel of the illegitimacy argument is that if the members of the UN do not perceive the council as being legitimate, it loses its capacity for effective action. Perceptions of illegitimacy held by an influential group of member-states, for instance, might result in the council struggling to gain support for its resolutions or may impede the council in making strong decisions.[3] Legitimacy is most pertinent when conferred by influential member-states and, more importantly, the parties to a conflict or situation themselves.[4] Indeed, by recognizing the council as a legitimate institution, the parties are acknowledging that the council has a part to play in the resolution of their situation. When a party recognizes the council as legitimate, it can be expected that behaviors exhibited might be reflective of this recognition. For instance, a party might request the assistance of a UN mediator or grant its consent for the deployment of a peacekeeping operation. For the council, legitimacy is generated by an intricate set of processes (theorized by Inis Claude, Ian Hurd, Bruce Cronin, David Caron, and Ian Johnstone). It can be argued that a host of sources, contributes to, or deducts from, the legitimacy of the council. These sources of legitimacy include (1) deliberation, (2) proceduralism, (3) performance, (4) standards and (5) consistency. It is worth examining each source individually.

Deliberation

Hurd and Cronin "conclude simply that deliberation – understood as the opportunity for participation and voice according to known procedures – legitimises outcomes."[5] It follows that if a member-state is included in the process of making a decision, the state will likely accept that decision as being legitimate. Deliberation is both a socializing and informational force. That is, deliberation acts to encourage alignment and reduce clashes of interest. Careful consideration of an agenda item works to improve outcomes through the dispersion of information. In sum, the argument can be made that "improving the quality of the deliberations would enhance the legitimacy and, therefore, effectiveness of Council decision making."[6]

Proceduralism

Adherence to the rules of the game credits the council in terms of procedural legitimacy. The procedures of the council were adopted under Article 30 of the charter, and are known as the Provisional Rules of Procedure of the Security Council (1983). The rules of the game, laid down in the provisional rules of procedure, "must be applied fairly and consistently for maximum legitimisation effect."[7] The procedures of the institution do not need to be fair per se. They may implicitly benefit the powerful. But they must be fairly applied. The council cannot deviate from or contravene the internal procedures of the UN. If it were to disregard its procedures, it would face diminished legitimacy in the eyes of its audience.

Purposive and performance legitimacy

In the previous chapter, council responsibility and purpose were discussed at length. It has been established that the purpose of the council is to maintain international peace and security. It is theorized, that if the social purpose of the council is accepted as appropriate by the organization's membership, and that the "broader norms and values of the society" are consistent with that purpose, then what is created is purposive legitimacy.[8] There clearly exists a strong connection between the social purpose of the organization and its substantive goals. The council's legitimacy will likely be enhanced if "it is seen to resolve crises of international peace and security."[9]

The goal model defines the concept of organizational effectiveness as "the degree to which an organisation achieves its goals," with a goal being defined as "a desired state of affairs which the organisation attempts to realise."[10] Sociologist Max Weber supported this idea when he wrote of an organization being directed towards "purposeful activity of a specified kind."[11] When considering the council, a concept of effectiveness seems a profoundly incoherent notion to grapple with— both difficult to define and difficult to measure. As Hurd and Cronin suggest, "there is no single passage in the charter which defines how the effectiveness of the council should be measured."[12] Despite the absence of a defined standard, most would concede that member-states, civil society, and the general public still hold an innate understanding of effectiveness. It has been suggested by Edward Luck that, "making a difference to the maintenance of international peace and security"[13] constitutes the ultimate test of council performance. Luck's suggestion is drawn from the charter—a clear starting point when examining the question of effectiveness. In Chapter V, Article 24 (1), the council's responsibility is defined: "In order to ensure prompt and effective action by the United Nations, its Members confer on the Security Council primary responsibility for the maintenance of international peace and security, and agree that in carrying out its duties under this responsibility the Security Council acts on their behalf."[14]

The council's responsibility is the "maintenance of international peace and security."[15] The wider membership assigned this responsibility to council to ensure prompt and effective action. For the council, the fulfillment of this responsibility is the reason for which the council exists—that is its purpose. It follows that the situational or operative goals of the organization will be reflective of the organization's purpose. When the council designates a threat to international peace and security, it is making an inference—the situation in question is undesirable. Hence, the council acts with the intention of remedying the situation. If the membership of the UN acknowledges the council as having achieved its goals, this perception of effectiveness can be credited to the body as performance legitimacy. The process of performance legitimization is by its very nature circular, as the council will only be seen as legitimate if it is also seen as effective.

Double standards, lax standards

The council has at times applied different sets of principles when dealing with similar situations—this is the very definition of double standards. The legitimacy of the council is adversely affected when it acts in one instance and fails to act in another, or when it acts with resolve in response to a particular event and then responds in a weak-willed manner to another. In the past, and at present, the council has been shown to obsess over certain situations such as Iraq (establishing a sophisticated sanctions regime—oil for food), while almost entirely neglecting others such as Rwanda (failing to prevent the genocide of 800,000 Tutsi and moderate Hutu). The council's weaknesses are shown up at these times. The inconsistency of the council should not be equated with prudent selectivity, however. Dominik Zaum and Adam Roberts have rightly argued that the selective nature of the council's brand of crisis management is "important, perhaps even desirable", as "it may reduce the danger of UN over-commitment."[16]

Likewise, the use of the veto can contribute to diminishing returns vis-à-vis legitimacy. The veto can be especially damaging when the vast majority of the general membership expects, or even demands, council action. Vetoes exercised against an overwhelming majority (i.e. 13–2 or 14–1 votes) only serve as an illustration of unchecked power, a power the vast majority of member-states would be in favor of abolishing. The frequent use of the veto by the United States to shield Israel from condemnatory resolutions have seen as a bone of contention for the vast majority of the membership. Russian and Chinese vetoes on Syria have been viewed in overwhelmingly negative terms.

Similarly, the application of lax standards discredits the council and adversely affects its legitimacy. The most striking fault has been the council's handling of a host of due process issues that have emerged around the imposition of targeted sanctions established under resolution 1267. It was successfully argued in the case of Yasin al-Qadi in the European Court of Justice that the regime amounted to "a 'denial of legal remedies' for the individuals and entities concerned, and is untenable under principles of international human rights law."[17] The case forced the council to examine the mechanisms of the discredited sanctions regime for fear of its possible collapse.

Mobilization

> The Achilles heel of the UN Security Council, the sine qua non, is the need for political will and political agreement. Only if Council members—and above all the permanent five (P-5) with the veto—can agree on the need for action, and the form of action, can that body function as intended.[18]

Most member-states do not possess the necessary capacity or the will to act unilaterally. Member-states will rarely commit to intervention abroad without first establishing "company"[19] because of the costs incurred—both political and financial. Multilateral forums, such as the Security Council allow for the establishment of such "company."[20] In the UN system, resources are pooled and costs shared, which in turn lowers the threshold for action. Generating the critical mass to drive action in the council is not a proven formula, but a complex and fluid confluence of dynamics. To assemble, marshal, or coordinate member-states requires one key ingredient: political will. As a former permanent representative explains:

> It [the Council] has a remarkable ability, if it wants to use that ability. So it is really an issue of willingness. The reason the Council doesn't solve problems, isn't because it can't, it's usually because it is unwilling to do so ... If the will is there the Council can do remarkable things.[21]

When engaged in political behavior, member-states need to demonstrate a willingness or motivation to expend resources. This is known as political will. Political will is a demonstration of a strong commitment and firm intention, on the part of member-states, to carry through a policy. Many, including Gareth Evans,[22] Nicolas Wheeler[23] and Kofi Annan[24] have argued that a manifest lack of political will is a major impediment to action in many instances. However, few have engaged in a concentrated analysis of this element. Political will is about the mobilization of political support to firstly, generate responses and, secondly, sustain implementation. The council is constantly confronted with a large number of problems, all of which concern international peace and security and most of which warrant the council's attention. States are, nevertheless, inherently selective "when deciding whether or not to seek Council involvement in a conflict."[25] For the council to respond to a conflict, key decision-makers and thought leaders need to be convinced of the conflict's importance.[26] Once convicted of an issue's importance, motivated member-states are more likely expend diplomatic capital and resources to mobilize the support required to break inertia and incite council action. In the first instance, the imperative for action is determined through a mix of interconnected factors: national interests, values, the immediacy and severity of the crisis, the CNN effect, NGO advocacy, and public opinion.

- **National interests:** When determining a response, member-states largely make pragmatic decisions, guided sometimes by principle but most often by hard political considerations. Are our interests at stake? If yes, do we pursue an intervention through the council to protect those interests? Powerful states and regional powers will regularly work through the council to further their foreign policy aims, and "since the Council's particular significance lies in capacity to pass resolutions that are binding on all member-states, it puts the members of the Council in a unique position that allows for certain national interest policies to be pushed through more easily."[27] However, these aims are usually peripheral to their core foreign policy objectives. The council has become a rather convenient "dustbin" into which peripheral conflicts may be placed.[28] In this respect, the council holds significant utility. It gives states a multilateral interventionist option (with the benefits of burden-sharing and legitimacy), when unilateral options are deemed too far a stretch (for reasons of willingness and cost).
- **Values:** Former Australian Foreign Minister Gareth Evans coined the term "good international citizenship" to describe the "area of foreign policy in which community values most influence the pursuit of national interests."[29] In defining good international citizenship, Evans advocates the abandonment of narrowly defined

what does that mean

strategic interest and the "pursuit of enlightened self-interest," or what Hedley Bull referred to as, "purposes beyond ourselves."[30] It can be argued that member-states acting out the good international citizen role are also doing so out of self-interest: reputation, status, and reciprocity. Even lip-service appeals to collective interests have proven to "fare better than self-serving arguments."[31] For this reason, collective interests are forever used as cover for self-interested pursuits.

- **Immediacy and severity of the crisis:** Events on the ground create a natural impetus for action. Fierce fighting in one country is likely to raise concerns in the neighborhood. For example, the violent disintegration of Yugoslavia led to the most significant refugee crisis in Europe since World War II. In mid-1992, 2.3 million people had been displaced, with 400,000 refugees fleeing to Western Europe.[32] The severity and immediacy of the crisis in the Balkans pushed European countries to respond.

- **The CNN effect:** The 24-hour news cycle is said to apply pressure to decision- and policy-makers. Firstly, global real-time news media coverage acts as a policy accelerant—foreshortening the time used to develop a mature reaction to a crisis. Secondly, news media affects foreign policy priorities. Indeed, priorities are routinely reordered by "emotional, compelling coverage of atrocities or humanitarian agency crises."[33] In 1994, Charles Krauthammer, opinion writer for the *Washington Post*, suggested that what determined the American decision to use airpower against the Serbs in Bosnia was the power of images: "But history played little part in our [the US] decision to weigh in with air power over Sarajevo. The decision was made on the basis of TV pictures. What changed American policy was coverage of the massacre at the market."[34]

    Michael Mandelbaum argued that, under Clinton, the CNN effect created a penchant for humanitarian interventionism. He has maintained that US interventions in Bosnia, Haiti, and Somalia were thoughtless misadventures rather than prudent initiatives born of a shrewd judgement of genuine US interests.

- **Civil society advocacy:** Since the end of the Cold War, civil society advocacy has become influential in shaping council responses to crises. NGOs subtly, or sometimes rather unsubtly, nudge national governments in certain directions. They recommend policies, and mobilize public, issues-based campaigns. In recent times, the doctrine of the Responsibility to Protect (RtoP), which the council supports under resolution 1674, has become the leading advocacy tool for NGOs.

- **Public opinion:** Domestic politics and public opinion shape foreign policy issue salience. Cynically, if the public cares about an issue or crisis, politicians will too. The CNN effect and civil society advocacy plays a role in shaping public perceptions of a conflict or crisis.

The permanent members

Effective council responses are predicated on permanent membership alignment. Firstly, as each permanent member possesses the power of veto, council action can be blocked by any permanent member through the exercise its veto (which means *I forbid, I prohibit* in Latin). When cast, the veto can prevent action being taken on a matter that is clearly consistent with the social purpose of the council and the norms of international society. Thus, the veto can disable the council and undermine its effectiveness. An example of this occurrence has been the consistent use of the veto by the United States on the question of Palestine.[35] The use of the veto in this manner has prohibited the council from addressing the problem by any effective means.

Secondly, the veto forces the P-5 to secure artificial alignment through compromise. The problem lies in the fact that sometimes reaching an agreement can actually compromise the council's response to a problem and "might lead to the watering down of resolutions and statements until they become ambiguous or even meaningless.[36] This phenomenon is referred to as "lowest common denominator-ism."[37] It is a phenomenon that can also act to undermine the effectiveness of the council. An example of this phenomenon was seen in the case of Syria in early 2012. The council adopted a presidential statement,[38] which supported the Annan Peace Plan. However, the statement was watered down by France to accommodate the concerns of Russia and China. As the statement did not take the form of a resolution, it was decidedly weak and ultimately ineffectual.

Overall, the veto can be viewed metaphorically like a shadow cast across every interaction, deliberation, and decision. Lingering above all these consultations is the reality that if an agreement cannot be reached between the permanent five, then a veto is pending. It is not often used, but that does not mean that it cannot be used. Although the veto is seldom exercised, the threat of its use is ever-present, as explained by a former permanent representative: "there was not a country that didn't threaten a veto in the back room. This is not something that happens once in a blue moon. The usual thing is, 'well we can't live with that,' and that means 'push us and we'll veto it.'"[39]

Alignment is fundamentally difficult to secure because member-states hold to their narrow perceptions of short-term national interest.

These perceptions dictate a member-state's stance in council deliberations, in turn limiting alignment on issues of contention. Kofi Annan, in recognition of this fact argues that the Security Council is not "a forum for resolving differences" but a "mere stage for acting them out."[40] To better understand the perspectives of the P-5 and the natural troubles of alignment, one must understand strategic culture.

Strategic culture was a term coined by Jack Snyder when he assessed the differences in nuclear strategy and posture between the United States and the Soviet Union. He argued the idea that "culturally-specific attributes factor into the formation of a state's strategy."[41] Culturally-specific attributes might include historical experiences, the development of idiosyncratic political systems, and philosophical and religious thought, all of which have a bearing on the development of particular strategic cultures. Meyer defines strategic culture as "comprising the socially transmitted, identity-derived norms, ideas and patterns of behaviour that are shared amongst the most influential actors and social groups within a given political community, which help shape a ranked set of options for the community's pursuit of security and defense goals."[42]

The permanent members use the council to protect and project their national interests. These national interests may relate to the protection of an alliance, foreign investment ties, military ties or armament contracts, and/or overarching strategic interests. The P-5 are some of the most influential economies. Their interests in economic terms are therefore considerably broad. Moreover, the P-5 comprises five of the top six largest weapons exporters. In strategic terms, each of the permanent members maintains a specific sphere of influence and a range of strategically important relationships and even foreign military installations and bases. All these interests intersect to create a complex interplay, which must be negotiated through the council on every matter.

The requirement for alignment, however, should not be overstated. Disinterest among the permanent members makes alignment on all but the most contentious issues (i.e. Syria) relatively straightforward. The overwhelming majority of situations do not directly impact on the real interests of any of the P-5, and so activist lead countries stimulate action. These lead countries must convince the P-5 of the importance of the issue. An example of this can be seen in the deployment of the United Nations Multidimensional Integrated Stabilization Mission in Mali (MINUSMA), the potential up-scaling of the UN's presence in the Central African Republic (CAR), and the reinforcement of the United Nations Mission in Cote d'Ivoire (UNOCI) during the crisis of 2011. In all of these examples, a politically willing France took the lead and stirred a largely disinterested P-5 to green light council action.

Upon reviewing many of the cases of the last two decades (Haiti, Sierra Leone, Mali, CAR, Cote d'Ivoire, and Liberia), the mode described above emerges as the general blueprint for council action.

Leadership: Mobilizing for intervention

Fen Olser Hampson has argued that "only major powers have the resources and capacities to intervene in internal conflicts."[43] The great powers (the P-5), the middle powers, and the smaller supporting countries have, at various times, adopted leadership roles in particular situations. France is perhaps the most active, leading on Cote d'Ivoire, Mali and the Central African Republic. Countries with influence can mobilize resources, provide economic assistance, muster political-diplomatic support and even furnish military forces to augment UN operations. They act, in effect, as godfathers. One former UN Secretariat official argues the point along similar lines:

> I don't think that I'd go as far to say that you need a Security Council member to run the 'show', but you almost always need a Security Council member, probably one of the P-5, to be the lead country on the 'politics'. My view is that you need one powerful country, with a lot of influence to say, 'we're going to carry the load on this, we're not going to do it alone, but we're going to carry this one.'[44]

Typically, P-3 members (France, the UK, and the United States) have taken on a leadership or godfather role vis-à-vis conflicts within their spheres of influence—framing the council's responses, mobilizing military and diplomatic resources, and crafting resolutions (as the penholder). Yet, the godfather role can also be viewed as neo-colonialist, hegemonic, or downright exploitative. Adekaye Adebajo, in a criticism of French behaviors in Africa, has remarked that, "in much of Africa, France is still seen as a kind of pyromaniac fireman that does a lot of destabilizing, behaving often like a deranged poker player, shuffling around regimes."[45] France's "dubious" role in Rwanda for Operation Turquoise is a case in point.[46]

Good leadership, nevertheless, is a requirement to make things happen. Leaders mobilize political will and then harness this will to pursue desired goals. A leader might manage an issue by owning the politics—guiding a resolution through the processes of the council. Alternatively, a leader might guide the implementation of resolutions by furnishing resources—in the form of troop contributions or military matériel. They might do both, as the UK did in Sierra Leone. But leaders do not necessarily need to be P-5 members. The E-10 have proven worthy leaders on many council files.

One former permanent representative interviewed pointed to the "innovative and productive diplomacy" of those member-states that have a record for making constructive contributions—members like Norway, Singapore, New Zealand, Costa Rica, and Australia.[47] Smart members can play a leadership role through their active and engaged diplomats, "who are not trying to run the world."[48] Perhaps, the best example of a smart member "creating an opportunity to be effective,"[49] was Canada, during its 1999–2000 term. Before taking its seat in January 1999, Canada's Permanent Representative Robert Fowler, an astute diplomat with a keen knowledge of Africa, recognized an opportunity: "I thought that maybe there would be an opportunity to make a difference [in Angola]. That the stars, were reasonably aligned, and could be better aligned."[50]

After recognizing the opportunity, Fowler decided to take on the position of chairman of the Angolan sanctions committee (pursuant to resolution 864). Sanctions were first imposed in 1993, while an additional suite of sanctions targeting UNITA specifically were later imposed in August 1997. In spite of these long-standing measures, sanctions had limited effect. Fowler singlehandedly transformed the sanctions committee, immediately issuing a progress report in February 1999[51] and travelling to Europe and throughout Africa.[52] Soon after, the council authorized two independent panels of experts to investigate UNITA (National Union for the Total Independence of Angola) violations (resolution 1237). Throughout 1999, Fowler flew under the radar: "nobody paid any attention to what we were doing, which was wonderful, and therefore we could do it."[53]

Fowler, as the architect of the re-energized regime, oversaw the panel's most significant report, which was published in March 2000.[54] The report, known as the Fowler Report, had a dramatic impact. It was clear in its identification of the arms-for-diamonds schemes. It was undiplomatic in its naming and shaming those involved in supporting UNITA—including Joe and Ronnie De Decker, and the serving presidents of Togo and Burkina Faso, Gnassingbé Eyadéma and Blaise Compaoré. Fowler's report was hard-hitting due in part to the support afforded him by the Canadian government. The report resulted in the strengthening of sanctions under resolution 1295 and the establishment of a monitoring mechanism to improve the effectiveness of the sanctions regime and investigate violations.[55] Starved of diamond income and weapons, Jonas Savimbi was killed by the MPLA (People's Movement for the Liberation of Angola) Government in 2002. In sum, Fowler's work over a two-year period on the council provides an exemplar of effective leadership. Moreover, "Fowler showed that independent panels of experts could be used in an innovative way to make it possible for the Security Council to apply pressure to sanctions violators."[56] Fowler's intervention is illustrative of another critical element: personal agency.

Forming a response

The council confronts a wide range of problems, from instability in the eastern Democratic Republic of the Congo (DRC) to nuclear proliferation on the Korean Peninsula. The council works to address these situations by first generating and then implementing resolutions or outputs. The decisions of the council need to be compatible with the context to which they are applied. A resolution that only addresses the symptoms is akin to paddling upstream against a torrent of water. An output that denies, simplifies, or misjudges the facts on the ground is unlikely to effect a positive transition. An example of incompatibility is the UN's intervention in the DRC. Incompatibility, in this case, stems from the labeling of the situation as a post-conflict transition. In spite of this presumption, the conditions of negative peace have not existed in the Eastern provinces throughout the intervention (1999–present). The establishment of fundamental security has not been achieved due to poorly designed disarmament, demobilization, and reintegration (DDR) and security sector reform (SSR) programs;[57] the council's seemingly unyielding support for an ineffective and unprofessional Forces Armées de la République Démocratique du Congo (FARDC); and a corrupt, ineffective, and repressive Congolese government.[58] Moreover, the council has largely failed to incorporate a sufficient understanding of the root causes of the conflict into its outputs.[59] Unfortunately, the Congo is not unique. The incompatibility described above is symptomatic of many of the council's interventions.

On the other hand, outputs that address the underlying causes of a conflict are best-placed to bring about positive peace over the longer term. Regional, domestic, provincial, and local actors hold the key. If these actors are allied in their support peace efforts, then council efforts achieve greater penetration. An example of a compatible council output was the UN's intervention in Croatia (1995). This intervention was compatible because the council provided the UN Transitional Administration for Eastern Slavonia, Baranja and Western Sirmium (UNTAES) with a clear and unproblematic mandate. UNTAES could then act flexibly and in a robust fashion to combat threats to peace and security.

The Security Council's toolbox, drafting resolutions

The council's toolbox contains an assorted range of instruments intended for use in different contexts to different ends. The Security Council actually has a narrow range of instruments at its disposal, as one former permanent representative remarked:

> What has it got? It's got sanctions, Chapter VI, which is basically peacekeeping. Chapter VII—which is all necessary means—providing the countries use their militaries. There's not a lot else.[60]

Each instrument has an internal logic or a way of working. The operating logic and inherent utility of each of the instrument contained in the council's toolbox is examined in the tables below (Tables 2.1–2.5). When the council adopts a resolution, it is applying the use of one or more of its instruments. These formal resolutions are the most tangible products of the council—they can send signals, support peace efforts, condemn violence, call on member-states to cooperate, invoke sanctions, create peacekeeping missions or empower military action.[61] For the most part, the council utilizes its soft power to persuade particular actors. This soft power is wielded with reference to Chapter VI of the charter (consensualism). In certain situations the council authorizes the use of hard power to coerce defiant actors. This hard power is authorized with reference to Chapter VII of the charter. After the 2003 invasion of Iraq by the United States, Joseph Nye added a third term to this lexicon—smart power. Nye described smart power as "the ability to combine hard and soft power into a winning strategy."[62] An argument can be made that the smarter the council is in wielding its instruments, of soft and hard power, the more effective it will be.

As mentioned in chapter one, the council is responsible for the maintenance of international peace and security, and is therefore accountable for all the stages of the process: from when a decision is made to its implementation. This process involves sometimes considerable input from the UN Secretariat. The role of the Secretariat is important to consider, because it is the Secretariat that provides information and recommendations on which council decisions are based, and it is often the Secretariat that implements resolutions once they have been adopted. The relationship is represented as a feedback loop—with the Secretariat providing input (recommendations), while at the same time interpreting and then acting upon council outputs.

UN presence: Field missions

Dag Hammarskjöld advanced the notion of a UN presence: an impartial enterprise used to nudge parties toward modifying "their political behaviour from rigid to more tolerant."[63] In contemporary times, the term UN presence implies the deployment of a field mission—either political, peacekeeping or peacebuilding. Most of these missions are heavy (involving many thousands of UN troops and staff) and costly (anywhere up $1.2 billion annually).

Table 2.1 UN presence: Field missions

Mission Type	Description
Traditional Peacekeeping	Involves the deployment of lightly armed troops whose task it is to monitor and report on the disputant parties' adherence to a particular agreement, usually a ceasefire. A traditional peacekeeping force places itself between the disputant parties. This creates a buffer zone separating the parties' militaries, and situates the UN operation in the middle as an interpositional force.
Special Political Missions (SPMs)	SPMs are non-military missions with a confined focus. Usually SPMs render limited assistance to national governments on issues such as electoral and rule of law reforms.
Complex Peacekeeping	These interventions combine military and civilian tasks, which generally include: electoral organization, support and supervision; humanitarian relief operations, including the protection of access corridors; demobilization, disarmament and reintegration (DDR); security sector reform (SSR); and human rights and rule of law promotion.
Transitional Administrations	The most extensive style of intervention, in terms of an encroachment on national sovereignty, is the UN protectorate or state surrogate model. In these interventions, the UN assumes all the basic civil administrative functions of a national government, including policing, administration of the judicial system, and reconstruction of infrastructure.
Residual Peacebuilding	It has become common for the council to authorize transitions from multidimensional peacekeeping operations to smaller longer-term peacebuilding offices. These offices, handed off to the General Assembly and the Peacebuilding Commission, are designed to ensure the completion of residual peacebuilding tasks and to consolidate gains made toward long-term peace and stability.

Diplomatic

Diplomacy is about making deals. It is about finding solutions to conflict through peaceful means. The council's diplomatic overtures are usually polite, but sometimes direct and menacing. For the most part, Chapter VI of the charter is prism through which the council's diplomatic efforts (preventative and soft power diplomacy) are focused. However, the council has the power to exercise coercive diplomacy—threats and demands—under Chapter VII.

Sanctions

If demands are not heeded, sanctions are the next step in the council's chain of response. Sanctions exist "between words and war."[64] They can be employed to a variety of ends: conflict resolution, counterterrorism, non-proliferation, protection of civilians, and democratization.

Table 2.2 Diplomatic instruments

Instrument	Description
Remonstrance (and Demand)	Refers to an appeal, a request of the council. In the context of the council, a remonstrance is used as a form of influence, either a gentle reminder or an enforceable demand. A remonstrance is a form of words, no more, which does not carry the weight of action per se, but might accompany a threat (i.e. a specific or unspecific threat of Article 41 measures) to convey its significance.
Peacemaking	Encompasses the use of tools such as diplomacy and mediation to bring conflict to an end. The council initiates, or more often supports, peacemaking efforts under Chapter VI of the charter. Article 33 outlines the possible means through which peace can be encouraged—negotiation, enquiry, conciliation, arbitration, judicial settlement, report to regional agencies, or arrangements.
Preventative Measures (including Preventive Deployment)	The objective of prevention is simple—to prevent an initial outbreak of armed conflict or the escalation of an existing one. The council, being reactionary seldom acts before the fact. The only example of preventive deployment is the UN Preventive Deployment Force, which was deployed with a mandate to prevent the spread of the Balkans conflict into Macedonia.

Table 2.3 Sanctions

Sanction Type	Description
Comprehensive Economic Sanctions	The imposition of comprehensive sanctions can completely isolate a country internationally. Due to the interconnected nature of international commerce and trade, the imposition of economic sanctions can swiftly bring a country's economy to its knees. Moreover, diplomatic sanctions, the prohibition of cultural exchanges and sporting matches can effectively preclude a sanctioned country's citizenry from actively and formally participating in global life, only serving to further enhance the general feeling of isolation experienced in the sanctioned country.
Travel Bans and Assets Freezes	Targeted sanctions are designed to be more precise, and are targeted in such a way as to affect the finances and/or liberties of a targeted individual, company or non-government organization. This type of pressure applied specifically to targeted leaders, personally affects those making decisions. The logic of targeted sanctions being that when political elites are deprived of luxury goods, international travel, their assets and access to finances, they will defer to their own personal interests; and as a consequence abandon deviant policies and pursue compliance with Security Council demands.
Arms Embargoes	Arms embargoes are the most favoured of the sanctions tools used by the council. Such embargoes are designed to deny or restrict availability of weapons. The rationale being that limiting access to new weaponry and ammunition will limit the conflict itself.
Commodity Specific Sanctions	Commodity specific sanctions are designed to deny the sale of certain commodities. These types of sanctions are essentially a form of partial economic sanction, often directed at severing or at least curtailing the independent income streams of spoilers and governments, which sustain conflict—include oil, diamonds, and timber.

International Criminal Tribunals (ICT)

The failure to prevent mass atrocity crimes in Srebrenica and Rwanda created a well of guilt for the council. The perpetrators of these mass killings—7,000 in the enclave of Srebrenica (and other incidents across the former Yugoslavia) and 800,000 people in Rwanda—would be held accountable for their crimes. In 1993 and 1994, respectively, the council established international tribunals to prosecute those responsible. Within a decade the Rome Statute of a permanent International Criminal Court entered into force. The Statute grants (under Article 13 and 16) the Security Council to power to refer and defer cases.

The use of force

Under Chapter VII of the charter, the council is granted the authority to authorize the use of force. The founders envisaged a military staff committee providing "strategic direction of any armed forces placed at the disposal of the Security Council."[65] The Cold War put paid to charter processes vis-à-vis the use of force. Instead, international enforcement action was to be licensed by the council. In 1950, the council authorized the use of force against the Democratic People's Republic of Korea (DPRK). Resolution 83 delivered the enforcement edict in ambiguous terms: "members of the United Nations furnish such assistance to the Republic of Korea as may be necessary to repel the armed attack and to restore international peace and security in the area."[66] The resolution was implemented under the auspices of UN Command. In practice, assistance rendered to the Republic of Korea was placed under unified US command (resolution 84).

Implementation

The council is easily distracted by the many crises that demand its attention. As a consequence, issues on the agenda (or on the seizure list) only receive cyclical attention, usually in times of crisis. Increases in troop strength or subtle shifts in mandates typify the council's knee-jerk reaction to crisis. The overcrowded nature of the agenda creates a caravan affect. For a time, the crisis will hold the council's attention.

Table 2.4 International legal instruments

Instrument	Description
International Criminal Actions (including International Criminal Tribunals and International Criminal Court Referrals)	In recent years, the council has been actively engaged in the pursuit of international justice through the establishment of ad hoc international criminal tribunals (Yugoslavia and Rwanda), special hybrid courts (Sierra Leone and Lebanon) and referrals (Darfur and Libya) to the International Criminal Court (ICC).

Table 2.5 Use of force instruments

Instrument	Description
Multinational Force (MNF) and Single Nation Force Authorisation	Under this model, the council, as the legitimate authority in international politics, would empower a regional actor or a group of nations to undertake the implementation of a specific council set mandate. MNFs have been used often as stopgap measures, as there is the tendency for member-states to limit involvement in complex situations and to deploy risk-averse operations with narrow temporized mandates.
Coalitions of the Willing	The council, essentially, issues the license for the use of force, as the legitimate licenser. The council might place conditions upon the purpose and parameters of its use, broad or limited.

The caravan, however, promptly moves on to another crisis in another country.

In March 2013, the council was busy on the Congo authorizing a Force Intervention Brigade (FIB) to neutralize spoilers in the East of the country. The following month, the council was preparing for a UN intervention in Mali (MINUSMA) to address the Tuareg and Islamist takeover of the North of the country. In December 2013, the council was concerned with the crisis in South Sudan. On 24 December, the council acted quickly, doubling the troop strength of the UN Mission in South Sudan (UNMISS). In March 2014, the council responded to the crisis in the Central Africa Republic (CAR). This snapshot confirms the almost constant attentional shifts. Under these conditions, sustaining support for implementation is eternally troublesome.

Resourcing

For the council to implement its resolutions member-states are required to contribute resources. Each resolution has its own resourcing requirements, depending on the instrument(s) employed. In peacekeeping scenarios, member-states are required to contribute troops and materiel (i.e. armored vehicles, helicopters). In other scenarios, the resourcing requirements might be significantly less. All in all, the mobilization of resources to implement decisions is crucial to the realization of desired outcomes. The allocation of insufficient resources can act as significant constraint on the council's capacity to act in the world. Overstretch, funding shortfall, and under-resourcing are terms commonly used in reference to council operations. The examples are numerous. In October 2010, the Special Representative of the Secretary-General (SRSG) for Sexual Violence in Conflict, Margot Ahlstrom, remarked that MONUSCO (United Nations Organization Stabilization Mission in the Democratic Republic of the Congo) was "overstretched and under-resourced."[67] In another case, the then Under-Secretary-General (USG) for Peacekeeping Operations, Jean-Marie Guéhenno, told the council in February 2008 that UNAMID (United Nations–African Union Mission in Darfur) was "severely under-resourced" and that "the number of troops, police, and their enabling capabilities currently in the mission area were simply not sufficient."[68]

The council often positions peacebuilding programs at the center of its solutions, yet rarely ensures that these programs are properly funded. Vital programs such as security sector reform (SSR); disarmament, demobilization, and reintegration (DDR); truth and reconciliation commissions; rule of law; and judicial reforms normally lie outside the UN general budget and the UN peacekeeping budget. As a result of this funding arrangement, these programs enjoy no guaranteed funding. Instead, they rely on the voluntary contributions of multilateral and bilateral donors. In certain situations, underfunding of critical programs, such as the reintegration phase of DDR, has actually directly threatened the peace itself. Even though the council might "urge all states and international organisations to provide resources,"[69] its instructions are inconsistently heeded.

What determines the level of resourcing? It can be argued that political will is the main determinant for the level of resourcing. A clear lack of political will on the part of member-states is often reflected in a lack of resources provided to carry out council decisions. A comparison between the cases of arms embargo enforcement in Libya and Darfur provides evidence to support this argument. In 2011, the council adopted resolution 1970, which imposed an arms embargo on Libya. To enforce and monitor this arms embargo, NATO used its Standing Maritime Group 1 and Standing Mine Countermeasure Group 1. Later, NATO increased the level of resources provided to further support the enforcement of the arms embargo, under its Operation Unified Protector.[70] In 2004, the council adopted resolution 1556, which imposed an arms embargo on all non-government entities and individuals (later applied to all parties to the ceasefire) in Darfur.[71] Unlike Libya, no member-states offered resources to monitor and enforce the arms embargo. It can be surmised from the allocation of these resources that the council's Libyan arms embargo enjoyed a higher level of political support than its Darfur arms embargo.

Evaluation

As of the start of 2015, there were 78 individual items of which the council was actively seized. Of those items many are subject to mandatory council reporting and mandate cycles.[72] For the most part, the Secretary-General (Secretariat, de-facto) undertakes these evaluative processes: 90-day, six-month or yearly reporting cycles are the norm. The Secretary-General's reports typically update the council on the recent in country political and security developments and the performance of the UN's presence (whether that be a mission, field office or special envoy). The Secretary-General concludes his or her reports with a set of observations, as well as strategic assessment recommendations (i.e. the mandate in the forthcoming period should reflect these priorities). On the question of UNAMID (United Nations African Union Missions in Darfur), the council requested the Secretary-General to undertake a "detailed and forward-looking review of UNAMID's progress towards achieving its mandate."[73] Understanding why a mission might be floundering should be a routine task, but for the council critical evaluative reviews are a rarity.

Conclusion

This chapter has charted the typical workflow of the council, passing through the waypoints of legitimacy, mobilization, response, and implementation. It has been a winding path of sorts, but one that has elucidated the council's complex mechanics. Understanding how the council works points the way to its reform. Even though mundane and far removed from the debates on expansion and composition, the strengthening of the internal mechanics of the council constitutes reform—improving something for the better.

Notes

1 Ian Hurd and Bruce Cronin, "Conclusion: Assessing the Council's Authority," in *The UN Security Council and the Politics of International Authority*, eds. Ian Hurd and Bruce Cronin (Abingdon: Routledge, 2008), 206.
2 Hurd and Cronin, "Introduction," in *The UN Security Council and the Politics of International Authority*, 6.
3 David D. Caron, "The Legitimacy of the Collective Authority of the Security Council," *American Journal of International Law* 87 (1993): 552–588.
4 If peripheral actors do not hold to perceptions of legitimacy, the effectiveness of the Council is not likely to be influenced.
5 Hurd and Cronin, "Introduction," in *The UN Security Council and the Politics of International Authority*, 8.

6   Ian Johnstone, "Legislation and Adjudication in the UN Security Council: Bringing Down the Deliberative Deficit," *American Journal of International Law 102*, no. 2 (2008): 275.

7   Hurd and Cronin, "Introduction," in *The UN Security Council and the Politics of International Authority*, 9.

8   Hurd and Cronin, "Introduction," in *The UN Security Council and the Politics of International Authority*, 6.

9   Hurd and Cronin, "Introduction," in *The UN Security Council and the Politics of International Authority*, 11.

10 Allen C. Bluedorn, "Cutting the Gordian Knot: A Critique of the Effectiveness Tradition in Organizational Research," *Sociology and Social Research* 64 (1980): 477–496.

11 Max Weber, *The Theory of Social and Economic Organization* (New York: The Free Press, 1997), 151.

12 Hurd and Cronin, "Introduction," in *The UN Security Council and the Politics of International Authority*, 11.

13 Edward C. Luck, *The UN Security Council: Practice and Promise* (Abingdon: Routledge, 2006), 5.

14 UN Charter, Chapter V, Article 24 (1).

15 UN Charter, Chapter V, Article 24 (1).

16 Adam Roberts and Dominik Zaum, *Selective Security: War and the United Nations Security Council since 1945* (Abingdon: Routledge-IISS, 2009).

17 Bardo Fassbender, *Targeted Sanctions and Due Process* (New York: Office of Legal Affairs, 2006)

18 David P. Forsythe, *The UN Security Council and Human Rights: State Sovereignty and Human Dignity* (Berlin: Friedrich Ebert Stiftung, 2012), 2.

19 Anonymous Interviewee, Interview with Author, June 2011.

20 Anonymous Interviewee, Interview with Author, June 2011.

21 Anonymous Interviewee, Interview with Author, June 2011.

22 Gareth Evans, *Responsibility to Protect: Ending Mass Atrocity Crimes Once and for All* (Washington, DC: Brookings Institute, 2008), 223.

23 Nicolas J. Wheeler, *Saving Strangers: Humanitarian Intervention in International Society* (New York: Oxford University Press, 2001).

24 "We have the means and the capacity to deal with our problems, if only we can find the political will." Kofi Annan, cited in Kel Currah, "MDGs 2.0 – An Open-sourced Campaign." http://www.eadi.org/typo3/fileadmin/MDG_2015_Publications/Currah_THINKPIECE.pdf.

25 Roberts and Zaum, *Selective Security.*

26 In the council, the representatives of the P-5 are critical. Outside the council, the leaders of these countries are critical. Other respected world leaders might also be considered key decision-makers, or at the very least, advocates for a response.

27 Sabine Hassler, *Reforming the UN Security Council Membership: The Illusion of Representativeness* (Abingdon: Routledge, 2013), 88.

28 Roberts and Zaum, *Selective Security.*

29 Gareth Evans, *Foreign Policy and Good International Citizenship,* 1990. http://www.gevans.org/speeches/old/1990/060390_fm_fpandgoodinternationalcitizen.pdf

30 Gareth Evans, *Foreign Policy and Good International Citizenship.* See also, Gareth Evans, *The Hard Headed Case for Good International Citizenship,*

2015. http://www.internationalaffairs.org.au/australian_outlook/the-hard-he
aded-case-for-good-international-citizenship/

31 Ian Johnstone, *The Power of Deliberation: International Law, Politics and Organizations* (New York: Oxford University Press, 2011), 16.

32 Henry Kamm, "Yugoslav Refugee Crisis Europe's Worst Since 40's," *New York Times*, 24 July 1992. http://www.nytimes.com/1992/07/24/world/yugo slav-refugee-crisis-europe-s-worst-since-40-s.html

33 Steven Livingston, *Clarifying the CNN Effect: An Examination of Media Effects According to the Type of Military Intervention* (Boston, Mass.: The Joan Shorenstein Center, 1997), 2.

34 Charles Krauthammer, "Intervention Lite: Foreign Policy by CNN," *Washington Post*, 18 February 1994. http://www.washingtonpost.com/archive/op inions/1994/02/18/intervention-lite-foreign-policy-by-cnn/42cffee5-62f8-46fd -82b3-5f9aba4a963b/

35 The US has exercised its veto in accordance with the Negroponte Doctrine.

36 Sydney Bailey and Sam Daws, *The Procedure of the UN Security Council (3rd Edition)* (New York: Oxford University Press, 1998), 228.

37 A term used by anonymous interviewee, July 2011.

38 Security Council Presidential Statement (S/PRST/2012), 21 March 2012.

39 Anonymous Interviewee, Interview with Author, June 2011.

40 Kofi Annan, *In Larger Freedom: Towards Security, Development and Human Rights for All* (New York: United Nations, 2005), 43.

41 Wilhelm Mirow, *Strategic Culture Matters: A Comparison of German and British Military Interventions since 1990* (Berlin: LIT Verlag Münster, 2009), 5.

42 Chistoph O. Meyer, *The Quest for a European Strategic Culture: Changing Norms on Security and Defence in the European Union* (London: St Martin's Press, 2006), 20.

43 Fen O. Hampson, "Third-Party Roles in the Termination of Intercommunal Conflict," *Millennium—Journal of International Studies* 26 (Dec): 729.

44 Anonymous Interviewee, Interview with Author, June 2011.

45 Adekeye Adebajo 2012, *"Peacekeeping in Africa" Book Launch at the International Peace Institute.* https://www.youtube.com/watch?v=G5GECFcG7o4

46 Adebajo 2012, *"Peacekeeping in Africa" Book Launch at the International Peace Institute.*

47 Anonymous Interviewee, Interview with Author, June 2011.

48 Anonymous Interviewee, Interview with Author, June 2011.

49 Robert Fowler, Interview with Author, June 2011.

50 Robert Fowler, Interview with Author, June 2011.

51 *Letter Dated 12 February 1999 from the Chairman of the Security Council Committee Established Pursuant to Security Council Resolution 863 (1993) Concerning the Situation in Angola* (Security Council document S/1999/ 147), 12 February 1999.

52 *Letter Dated 4 June 1999 from the Chairman of the Security Council Committee Established Pursuant to Security Council Resolution 863 (1993) Concerning the Situation in Angola* (Security Council document S/1999/644), 4 June 1999.

53 Robert Fowler, Interview with Author, June 2011.

54 Chairman of the Security Council Committee Established Pursuant to Security Council Resolution 863 (1993) Concerning the Situation in

42 *The agency of the UN Security Council*

Angola, *Report of the Panel of Experts on Violations of Security Council Sanctions against UNITA* (S/2000/203), 10 March 2000.
55 Security Council resolution 1295, 18 April 2000.
56 Alex Vines, "Monitoring UN Sanctions in Africa: The Role of the Experts Panels," in *Verification Yearbook*, ed. Trevor Findlay (London: Vertic, 2003), 251.
57 The Council hasn't insured the professionalism of the FARDC. It is known that the FARDC is part of the security problem.
58 Jessica Hatcher and Alex Perry 2012, *Defining Peacekeeping Downward: The U.N. Debacle in Eastern Congo,*http://world.time.com/2012/11/26/defining-peacekeeping-downward-the-u-n-debacle-in-eastern-congo/.
59 Complex overlay of regional, national and local conflict: Séverine Autesserre, *The Trouble with the Congo: Local Violence and the Failure of International Peacebuilding* (New York: Cambridge University Press, 2010).
60 Anonymous Interviewee, Interview with Author, June 2011.
61 Ian Hurd, *After Anarchy: Legitimacy and Power in the United Nations Security Council* (Princeton, N.J.: Princeton University Press, 2007), 3.
62 Joseph Nye 2006, "In the Middle East, the Goal Is 'Smart Power,'" *Boston Globe,*19 August 2006. http://belfercenter.hks.harvard.edu/publication/1590/in_mideast_the_goal_is_smart_power.html
63 Peter B. Heller, *The United Nations under Dag Hammarskjold, 1953–1961* (Latham, Md.: Scarecrow Press, 2001), 38.
64 Loraine Sievers and Sam Daws, *The Procedure of the UN Security Council* (Oxford: Oxford University Press, 2014), 519.
65 UN Charter, Chapter VII, Article 47 (3).
66 Security Council resolution 83, 7 July 1950.
67 RFI, "DRC Army Raping and Killing, Says UN Envoy," *RFI*, 15 October 2012. http://www.english.rfi.fr/africa/20101015-drc-army-raping-and-killing-says-un-envoy
68 United Nations, *African Union-United Nations Hybrid Force in Darfur Severely under-Resourced to Protect Civilians, Peacekeeping Chief Warns Security Council*, 2008. http://www.un.org/press/en/2008/sc9243.doc.htm.
69 Security Council resolution 1260, 20 August 2000.
70 Twelve countries participated in the maritime operation, which included 18 frigates and five destroyers.
71 "All States shall take the necessary measures to prevent the supply of arms and related materiel of all types and also of technical training and assistance in relation to actors operating in Darfur" (res. 1556).
72 United Nations Department of Political Affairs, *Security Council Reporting and Mandate Cycles*, 2015. http://www.un.org/en/sc/inc/pages/pdf/sccycles.pdf.
73 Security Council resolution 2113, 30 July 2013.

3 Reform

- **The dynamics and dimensions of Security Council reform**
- **G4 nations (new permanency)**
- **Uniting for Consensus (UfC)**
- **Africa (C-10)**
- **L-69**
- **The Permanent Five**
- **Civil society proposals**
- **Conclusion**

This chapter will provide a flyover of the reform debate. It will begin with a recap of sorts, an examination of the charter and the intentions of its drafters. This exercise will be ordered using several of the five key reform issues: the categories of membership; the size of an enlarged Security Council; the working methods of the council; the question of the veto; and regional representation. The second section of the chapter will map the narrative of reform: from Razali via Annan and the high level panel, and finally the intergovernmental negotiations. Thereafter, the chapter will explore the internal logic of the various reform proposals, as well as the intentions and perspectives of the key proposers and their respective blocs.

The dynamics and dimensions of Security Council reform

In 1944, at the home of Robert Woods Bliss in Dumbarton Oaks (Washington, DC), the Soviets, the Americans, and the British drew up the plans for the UN Security Council. The original thoughts of the drafters of Chapters V through VIII are interesting points of reference in the context of the present reform debate.

*The categories of membership and size of an enlarged Security Council
and working methods of the council*

All the great powers present (the UK, the USSR, China, and the
United States) at Dumbarton Oaks naturally agreed that they each
would occupy permanent seats on the council. France and Brazil were
the only question marks. While Churchill was committed to France,
FDR showed a commitment to Brazil. In the end, a "charming but
weak"[1] France was included on the body after the USSR dropped its
objections. The delegates knew it would be necessary to include smaller
powers on the council as elected members. FDR insisted on an ample
number of elected members, Stettinius opted for the term "suitable."[2] All
recognized that an appropriate number of elected seats were required "to
guarantee support for the organization among the second and third
rank of nations."[3] The three primary participants at Dumbarton Oaks held
different opinions on the term limits of elected members. The British
preferred three-year terms, the Soviets favored two, and the Americans
only one. The British and the Americans compromised, and opted for "two
year terms with rotating retirement."[4]

On the question of size, the British delegation spelled out the
dilemma in very clear terms: efficiency versus support. If the council
were smaller, then it would be more efficient. However, if it were too
small, it would not garner sufficient support among the smaller powers.
In the end, the delegates decided that six elected members would
accompany the five permanent veto-wielding members on an 11-seat
council. The elected six would hold the majority, as well as a de-facto
sixth veto (if voting together against all five permanent members). The
first session of the General Assembly was attended by 51 member-
states, which translated into a General Assembly membership to
council membership ratio of about 5 to 1 (51:11).

The question of the veto

The most troublesome discussions at Dumbarton Oaks concerned the
question of the veto. The great powers had no trouble answering the question of whether or not they should each be granted the privilege of the
veto. Ultimately, the permanent members were the nations most capable
of providing the new organization with a military backbone. For this
reason, they argued that they should hold the final say on where and
when those forces would be deployed. The organization would fail if
the support and resources of the great powers were not forthcoming.
The rights of the smaller powers would be subjugated to the needs of

great power unity—a trade that all were willing to make, albeit begrudgingly. Furthermore, offering the privileges of an exclusive veto power was also the one way by which the great powers could be bound to the organization.

The delegates were then confronted by an inescapable conundrum: what if a permanent member was involved in a dispute? In such an event, would that great power be prepared to relinquish its veto and throw itself on the mercy of the council (to be bound by its decisions)? It was suggested that the great powers, especially the USSR and the US, were simply far too militarily powerful to be subject to the enforceable decisions of the council. They would likely ignore its decisions and leave the organization, as was commonplace in the League. Japan, Germany, and Italy all withdrew from the League after facing the condemnation of their peers. An absolute veto would only subject the smaller powers to the law, while placing the permanent veto-wielding members above it, so to speak.

On the other hand, some argued for veto limitation on disputes involving the great powers. The proponents of veto limitation argued that the source of the league's impotence was its inability to adequately deal with naked aggression on the part of its most powerful members. Surely, if a great power were to defy the council, they would be drawn into a seemingly inevitable conflict with the UN. Any such conflict would see the forces of the just and principled UN against a recalcitrant great power. As a result of veto limitation, great powers might modify their behaviors to avoid entanglements that might attract the council's attention. The arguments for absolute veto and qualified veto were both compelling. But would the smaller powers accept the absolutist proposition? Alexander Cadogan, for one, felt that the proposition was untenable and that an absolute veto would simply not be accepted by the smaller powers. Article 27 (3) sets out the veto compromise: "in decisions under Chapter VI, and under paragraph 3 of Article 52, a party to a dispute shall abstain from voting."[5]

In practice, the Article is a virtual dead letter. No member of the council has abstained under Article 23 (3) since Argentina refrained from voting on resolution 138 (1960), which concerned the capture of Adolf Eichmann in Buenos Aires by Israeli Mossad agents without the knowledge of the Frondizi Administration.

Regionalism

Regionalism loomed large in wartime discussions between the allied leaders. Churchill spoke of a Council of Europe and a Council of Asia in 1943, and it was said that FDR too was in favor of a regional approach. Chapter VIII of the charter laid down the basic parameters for the regional arrangements. Regional organizations could exist, but would be made nominally subordinate to the council. The arrangements allowed the council to call upon regional organizations to undertake enforcement action under its authority, while precluding enforcement action taken without the council's express authorization.

Regionalism was not an overriding criterion upon which the selection of permanent members would be made. Yet, the ROC was neither seen as a great power at the time nor a potential great power. FDR, nevertheless, viewed the regime of Chiang Kai-shek as a potential counterweight to Japan in East Asia. These decisions reinforce the view that the allocation of permanent seats was made on a pragmatic basis rather than on any preference for regionalism.

Expansion in the 1960s

By the 1960s, the organization's membership had doubled, partly as a result of the UN's decolonization efforts. India, as the champion of the Non-Aligned Movement (NAM) led a chorus of voices calling for an enlargement of the council. In 1965, these calls were heeded and the council was enlarged to 15, incorporating a further four elected members [a representation ratio of 8 to 1 (117:15)]. The P-5, however, were somewhat lukewarm on the proposed changes. France and the Soviet Union voted against the GA resolution; the United Kingdom and the United States abstained, while the ROC voted in favor. Despite Soviet objections, resolution 1991 (A) was adopted with the support of a large majority of the assembly, which included virtually every member outside the Soviet bloc (97 yeses; 11 nos; 4 abstentions). The resolution called upon "all member-states to ratify ... the amendments"[6] by the deadline of 1 September 1965. At this juncture, the Soviets could have easily vetoed expansion (by failing to ratify the resolution). Yet surprisingly they were among the first to deposit their instrument of ratification to the UN. Subsequently, no account was offered explaining the dramatic "reversal of its position."[7]

Resolution 1991 (A) made four amendments to the charter. It also altered the electoral groupings by which members of the General Assembly could be elected to the council. The original council, with its six elected seats, drew its membership from five electoral groupings: two seats for Latin America, one each from the British Commonwealth, Western Europe, Asia/Eastern Europe, and the Middle East. The ten elected seats of the new post-1965 council were to be divided between five electoral groupings: five seats for Africa and Asia, one for the Eastern Europe Group (EEG), two for the Western Europe and Others Group (WEOG), and two for the Latin American and Caribbean Group (GRULAC). Since the expansion in 1965, the council has essentially remained in stasis, altered only to allow the People's Republic of China (PRC) to replace the ROC in 1971, and the Russian Federation to replace the Soviet Union in 1992. These alternations were nevertheless made without charter amendment (under Article 108). To this day, Article 23 still contains the USSR and the ROC among the list of permanent members.

Calls for renewal in the 1990s

The Cold War freeze began to lift in the late 1980s and a spirit of great power cooperation broadened the scope of council action. From 1946 to 1990 the council adopted a total of 646 resolutions, an average of 14 resolutions a year. Over the 10-year period from 1990 the council's output, in resolutions, increased by 450 percent (to an average of 63 resolutions a year). The council was doing more, in more places. The hyperactivity of the council led to calls for renewal. In 1994, Razali Ismail of Malaysia was made chair of the Open-Ended Working Group on the Question of Equitable Representation on and Increase in the Membership of the Security Council and Other Matters related to the Security Council (also dubbed "the never-ending working group"). In 1997, Razali put forward a plan for renewal, in the form of a draft General Assembly resolution. The plan envisaged a 24-member council, which would include five new permanent members without veto and four new elected seats (one each for Africa, Asia, Eastern Europe, and Latin America). Moreover, the P-5 would retain their veto, but would be circumscribed as to its use (only applying to Chapter VII matters). In late 1998, the draft was rejected because it could not garner the two-thirds majority assent required.

Razali believed, perhaps wrongly, that only a simple majority would be required to fundamentally alter the charter. Clearly, the changes earmarked required charter amendment made in accordance with the three-stage process outlined in Article 108:

Amendments to the present Charter shall come into force for all Members of the United Nations when they have been adopted by a vote of two thirds of the members of the General Assembly and ratified in accordance with their respective constitutional processes by two thirds of the Members of the United Nations, including all the permanent members of the Security Council.[8]

Firstly, two-thirds of the membership (129 of 193 members) must support the amendment, which takes the form of a resolution in the General Assembly. Secondly, the stipulations of the resolution must then be ratified by the parliaments of two-thirds of the membership. This is due to the fact that the charter is a constituent treaty, which has the potential to bind its signatories. Thirdly, the parliaments of all five permanent members must ratify the charter amendment if the amendment is to be carried.

The crux of the impasse was, and remains, based on a rather simple interest-based equation: one bloc gains power, while another potentially loses it. The winners of reform through expansion would be those states that feel that they are entitled to a permanent seat on the council, namely the Group of Four (G4): Japan, Germany, India, and Brazil. The losers of reform by way of new permanency would be the regional rivals of the aspirants (Pakistan and Argentina), the future aspirants (South Korea, Mexico, and Turkey), and the principled middle powers (Canada and Spain). Clearly, any reform package must pass the interest test for virtually all but the most principled states. Diplomats using a series of political calculations ask the obvious question: does the reform package currently on the table serve the best interests of my country?

Models A and B

At the Millennium Summit (2000) the international community again resolved, "to intensify [its] efforts to achieve a comprehensive reform of the Security Council in all its aspects."[9] In 2003, Annan appointed a High Level Panel on Threats, Challenges and Change. The panel's report—A More Secure World: Our Shared Responsibility—affirmed a set of reform principles and presented two models for the membership's consideration. Firstly, reform should seek the enhanced involvement of "those who contribute most to the United Nations financially, militarily and diplomatically."[10] Secondly, reform should address the representative imbalance between states of the global north and the global south. Thirdly, reform should not impede the effectiveness of the council. Finally, reform should make the council a more democratic and accountable body.

The two proposed models used four continental blocs (Africa, Europe, the Americas, and Asia) instead of the five standard electoral groupings. Model A imagined a council of 24 members. This model roughly aligned with the G4 approach. The five permanent members would remain in place with their vetoes intact, while an additional six permanent members would join the council, but without veto power. In terms of additional members (translated into the five electoral groups), the model allocated two permanent and one elected seat to Africa; two permanent and one elected seat to Asia; one permanent to WEOG (Western Europe and Other Group); and one permanent and two elected seats to the Americas. The EEG (Eastern Europe Group) would remain unaltered (see Table 3.1).

Model B also envisaged a 24-seat council. This model roughly aligned with the Uniting for Consensus (UfC) approach. The P-5 would remain and no new permanent seats would be established. Instead, a new type of seat would be created: a four-year renewable seat. The model assigned two renewable seats to all four regions, while giving Africa an extra elected seat (see Table 3.2).

Kofi Annan's response to the panel was captured in the 2004 report, *In Larger Freedom*. On the matter of council reform, he reiterated the

Table 3.1 Model A translated into current UN electoral groupings

Groupings	Elected	New Permanent	Permanent
WEOG	1 (-1)	1	3 (US, UK, France)
Asia-Pacific	3 (+1)	2	1 (China)
Africa	4 (+1)	2	–
Eastern Europe	1	–	1 (Russia)
GRULAC	4 (+2)	1	–
TOTAL	13	6	5

Table 3.2 Model B translated into current UN electoral groupings

Groupings	Elected	4-Year Renewable	Permanent
WEOG	2	1 or 2	3
Asia-Pacific	2	2	1
Africa	4 (+1)	2	–
Eastern Europe	1	1 or 0	1
GRULAC	2	2	–
TOTAL	11	8	5

panel's recommendations, while urging the membership to "agree to take a decision"[11] on the issue prior to the Millennium+5 Summit in September 2005. Despite Annan's best efforts, no agreement could be reached in 2005, or at any time since. As Luck rightly observed "political convergence precedes institutional change."[12] Quite simply, Annan's plans denied the historical tug-of-war over reform. Reform was now viewed as an event and not a process.[13] Prior to the summit, three blocs put forward their proposals in the form of draft General Assembly resolutions: the UfC (A/59/L.68), the G4 (A/59/L.64), and the Africans (A/59/L.67). The moment for reform had arrived. The G4 were supremely confident, but also unwilling to compromise. It was reported that the UfC were prepared to accept 10-year seats. The G4, however, were not prepared to meet them halfway. The mix of confidence and contention ultimately killed the summit process, as both sides retreated into their defensive positions. In September 2007, a group of members proposed a draft resolution (A/61/L.69). The draft resolution never proceeded to a vote, but its introduction precipitated a change in the chair of the working group's progress report.[14] It is also became the rallying point for a new cross-regional group from the global south—the L-69.

Intergovernmental Negotiations on Security Council Reform (IGN)

On 15 September 2008, the continued stalemate on reform entered a new phase with the creation of the IGN (decision (62/557)). In early 2009, the GA president appointed Zahir Tanin, the Permanent Representative for Afghanistan, to serve as the chairman of the process. Tanin and the various presidents of the General Assembly nobly attempted to drive the process forward, as round after round of the negotiations wore on. If one initiative failed to gain traction, the General Assembly leadership adopted another, and then another. Firstly, in 2010, Zanin forwarded a negotiation text to delegations. The annex to the document summarized a total of 30 proposals from member-states and the various blocs. Over the course of several rounds of negotiations, the text itself underwent three revisions. Secondly, during the eighth round of negotiations (in late 2011), the blocs again introduced draft resolutions reflecting their positions. Thirdly, in late 2013, the Advisory Group created by president of the GA provided a non-paper, a "set of ideas pertaining to the negotiations."[15] Fourthly, Tanin decided to formulate a set of proposals, as is the prerogative of the chair of most UN committees.

The repetitious nature of the negotiations, the lack of a spirit of compromise, and the use of procedural maneuvers stymied the process and inhibited the realization of a true negotiating text. In short, Security Council reform had become a mirror of the intractable conflicts the council itself dealt with (i.e. Cyprus, Western Sahara, and the Palestinian question). The membership had become enveloped by a haze of paperwork (letters, non-papers, revisions, draft resolutions), which only served to confuse. The complaint of the vice-chairpersons of the president of the General Assembly, in their report of 2008, provides an apt summation of the stubbornness by which the various interest groups conducted themselves throughout the deliberations:

> Positions among major interest groups have not moved significantly, despite stated expressions of disposition to act with flexibility and a general recognition that Security Council reform would necessarily require compromise.[16]

In his assessment, Tanin conceded that the limiting factor (for the IGN) was the commitment of member-states, or lack thereof: "it is time to recognize the limits of what can further be achieved within the current framework of the Intergovernmental Negotiations (IGN) without a deepened Member-state commitment to undertaking robust negotiations, involving active give and take."[17]

Courtenay Rattray, permanent representative of Jamaica, succeeded Tanin as chair of the IGN in late 2014. The appointment of the new chair and the approaching seventieth anniversary of the founding of the UN provided yet another false dawn for the process. Rattray's first intervention was the circulation of a framework document, which was intended to be "an evolving, working document on the road towards the creation of a draft negotiating text."[18] The membership was invited to make submissions to the framework document regarding five salient questions of the reform process. The lengthy document revealed the fact that no major shifts in the landscape had occurred. Only a handful of groups (including the G4, the Caribbean Community [CARICOM], C-10, L-69) and countries provided inputs into the framework. The Arab group, the UfC, China, Russia, and the US were all notable absentees.

On 11 September 2015, the General Assembly adopted a decision (A/69/L.92), by consensus, on the question of Security Council Reform. The decision was noteworthy, not for the fact that it was, in large part, a technical rollover, but because it made mention of the framework document (otherwise known as the "text and its annex circulated by the President of the General Assembly in his letter dated 31 July 2015").[19] The decision suggested that member-states build on the "positions of and proposals made by Member-states."[20] Reactions to the decision were wildly different. The G4 and L-69 hailed the "landmark decision."[21] The Indian delegate suggested that the decision had fundamentally altered the course of the reform debate: the negotiations were now on "an irreversible, text-based path."[22] On the other side of the debate, the UfC viewed the decision as a technical rollover from one session of the General Assembly to the next. Clearly, the blocs are not in agreement on whether the decision is actually substantive or not. Therefore, the only reasonable reading of the decision is: business as usual.

G4 nations (new permanency)

The G4 is comprised of Japan, Germany, India, and Brazil. Each member of the group seeks a permanent seat on the council. In a sense, the group is forged from a pact between its members to mutually support each other's bids for permanency. The G4 nations view themselves as the heirs apparent and favor a proposal that, if implemented, would see the council expanded to 25 seats. The concept of new permanency is prefaced on the notion that the current council does not reflect the geopolitical realities of the twenty-first century. In short, the council's permanent membership is outdated. To address the disequilibrium, the G4 proposes the inclusion of six new permanent seats and five new elected seats (see Table 3.3 for regional distribution of seats).

The proposed changes would create a permanent-eleven (P-11) and an elected fifteen (E-15). A G4 proposed article 23 (1) amendment might comprise the following language:

> The Security Council shall consist of twenty-five Members of the United Nations. Brazil, the People's Republic of China, France, India, Japan, Federal Republic of Germany, the Russian Federation, the United Kingdom of Great Britain and Northern Ireland, the United States of America, and [two Africa countries] shall be permanent members of the Security Council. The General Assembly shall elect fifteen other Members of the United Nations to be non-permanent members of the Security Council, due regard being specially paid, in the first instance to the contribution of Members of the United Nations to the maintenance of international peace and security and to the other purposes of the Organization, and also to equitable geographical distribution.[23]

The new permanent members would not, however, necessarily be granted the right to exercise the veto. In their communiqués, regarding

Table 3.3 The blocs, their members, and their supporters (supposed)

	Members	Supporters/Observers
G4		
Brazil	–	France, United Kingdom, Chile, Finland, Slovenia, Australia, South Africa, Vietnam, and the Phillipines
India	–	France, United Kingdom, a collection of countries in the Carribean, Central Asia, Northern Europe, Eastern Europe, Africa, the Middle East, and Latin America
Japan	–	France, United Kingdom, Australia, Pacific Islands Forum
Germany	–	France and United Kingdom
UfC	Argentina, Canada, Colombia, Costa Rica, Indonesia, Italy, Malta, Mexico, Pakistan, South Korea, San Marino, Spain, and Turkey	China
L-69	Barbados, Benin, Bhutan, Burundi, Cape Verde, Fiji, Grenada, Guyana, Haiti, India, Jamaica, Liberia, Mauritius, Nauru, Nigeria, Palau, Papua New Guinea, Rwanda, Saint Vincent and the Grenadines, Seychelles, Solomon Islands, South Africa, Tuvalu, Vanuatu	India and Brazil

	Members	*Supporters/Observers*
C-10	Algeria, Republic of the Congo, Equatorial Guinea, Kenya, Libya, Namibia, Senegal, Sierra Leone, Uganda, and Zambia	African bloc (54 nations)
ACT	Austria, Chile, Costa Rica, Estonia, Gabon, Hungary, Ireland, Jordan, Lichtenstein, New Zealand, Norway, Papua New Guinea, Peru, Portugal, Saudi Arabia, Slovenia, Sweden, Switzerland, and Uruguay	Tanzania

the extension of the veto, the G4 has stated that, "the new permanent members would not exercise the right of veto until the question of the extension of the right of veto to new permanent members has been decided upon the framework of a review conference."[24] There is nevertheless confusion surrounding several aspects of the proposal. Firstly, the proposed veto moratorium could be interpreted one of three ways:

1   The proposed charter amendment would grant veto rights to the new permanent members, in the first instance, but they would choose do not exercise these rights until after a future review conference.
2   A veto moratorium clause would be specified in any amendment to Articles 23 (1) and 27 (3). The extension of the veto would then be subject to the outcome of a review conference (15-years) and the deletion of the moratorium clause at a future date (i.e. requiring another amendment).
3   An amendment giving veto to the new permanent members would be made at a future review conference (15 years after reform). This interpretation of the language was confirmed by the G4 during discussions in May 2015.

Secondly, the two African permanent seats (to be chosen by the African Union membership) have yet to be designated. The G4 plans are therefore unlikely to find approval in Washington (either on Capitol Hill or at the White House). The following section profiles each of the

Table 3.4 The G4 nations preferred model

Groupings	Elected (+ New Elected)	New Permanent	Permanent
WEOG	2	1 (Germany)	3
Asia-Pacific	3 (+1)	2 (Japan and India)	1
Africa	4 (+1)	2 (as yet undecided)	–
Eastern Europe	2 (+1)	–	1
GRULAC	4 (+2)	1 (Brazil)	–
TOTAL	14	6	5

aspirant members of the G4, explaining the basis for their respective bids and the roadblocks that may thwart their efforts.

Japan

Japan formally surrendered to the Allied forces on 2 September 1945. One month later, the UN was founded. Like Germany, Japan remained an enemy of the organization under the enemy state articles of the charter (Articles 54 and 107), eventually being admitted to full membership in December 1956. One year later, Japan was elected to the Security Council.[25] Since then, Japan has served 10 terms (or a total of 20 years) on the council, the most of any elected member (together with Brazil).

Japanese foreign policy is partial to the UN. There are a number of reasons for this. Firstly, Japan's constitution is pacifist in nature, which accords with the spirit of the Preamble and Chapter VI of the charter. Article 9 of the Japanese Constitution states that "the Japanese people forever renounce war as a sovereign right of the nation and the threat or use of force as means of settling international disputes."[26] Secondly, Japan is not a member of any regional alliance structure (i.e. NATO) or security community (i.e. EU). The UN is, therefore, viewed as the prism through which Japan's multilateral engagement is focused. Thirdly, the UN enjoys bipartisan support in the Diet—with both the conservative Liberal Democratic Party (LDP) and the centrist Democratic Party of Japan (DPJ) supporting the UN. However, only 45 percent of the Japanese public views the UN favorably, while 40 percent hold an unfavorable view.

In objective terms, Japan is the third largest economy ($4.90 trillion GDP), tenth most populous country (127 million), with the seventh largest defense budget, and fourth largest Official Development Assistance

(ODA) contribution ($11.79 billion). Japan has exhibited a "preference for primary financial contributions to international peacekeeping and humanitarian programmes and actions under the auspices of the UN and other multinational groups."[27] Japan is the second largest contributor to both the UN general (12.53 percent) and peacekeeping budgets (10.83 percent), and hosts the United Nations University. Since the adoption of the Act on Cooperation for United Nations Peacekeeping Operations and Other Operations in 1992, Japan has also provided modest contributions to various UN missions including the United Nations Transitional Authority in Cambodia (UNTAC), the United Nations Disengagement Observer Force (UNDOF), the United Nations Mission of Support in East Timor (UNMISET), and most recently UNMISS (UN Mission in South Sudan).[28] In the council, the Japanese mission has championed working methods reforms and the issue of non-proliferation. Note 507, a Japanese diplomatic product, lent impetus to the campaign for working methods reform.

Japan's bid faces several potential obstacles. Firstly, Sino–Japanese relations present the largest stumbling block to the bid. Over recent years, disputes over the Senkaku-Diaoyu Islands in the East China Sea has elevated tensions between Tokyo and Beijing. Underlying the tensions is a historical mutual dislike brought on by the era of Japanese militarist imperialism. Both republics view the other in overwhelmingly negative terms: 90 percent of Chinese and 73 percent of Japanese hold a negative opinion of the other. Secondly, as Chapter VII of the charter invests the council with the sole authority to wage war, some view Article 9 of the Japanese constitution as a hurdle for Japan's bid. While at the US State Department, both Colin Powell and Richard Armitage argued that "it would be difficult for Japan to become a permanent UN Security Council member if it cannot play a greater military role for international peace."[29] In July 2014, the Japanese government decided to approve a reinterpretation of Article 9, a shift aimed at normalizing Japan's national defense. The reinterpretation allows Japan to exercise force if one of its allies is attacked (the right to collective self-defense). While allies including the US welcomed the policy change, both China and South Korea were critical of the move.

Germany

Germany was another of the "enemy states" of the UN. Following the war, the country was partitioned between the German Democratic Republic (DDR) in the East (Berlin) and the Federal Republic of Germany (BRD) in the West (Bonn). Both of the Germanys joined the UN on

18 September 1973. Upon reunification, BRD's seat at the UN continued, while the DDR's seat was dissolved. West Germany first served on the council in 1977, while East Germany served its only term from 1980–1981. West Germany served a second term between 1988 and 1989. Since reunification, Germany has occupied a WEOG seat three times (1995–1996, 2003–2004, and 2011–2012).

Germany's bid for a permanent seat on the council is premised on a number of facts. Germany is the third largest contributor to the UN, the fourth largest economy, and the powerhouse of Europe. Arguably, the most significant roadblock to Germany's bid is the EU dilemma. Currently, two other EU members (France and the United Kingdom) are permanent members of the council. If the council were expanded to reflect the G4's preferred model, it is possible that up to seven EU members could serve on the council at any one time.[30] As the Lisbon Treaty defines a common foreign and security policy for the EU, many have argued that a common EU seat would be a more logical approach to a European permanent seat. The German government appeared open to the possibility of a common EU seat, but only if France and the UK relinquished their seats. However, neither France nor the UK will countenance this prospect, at least not in the immediate future. Another potential roadblock is Germany's clear preference for EU and NATO engagement over the UN. In line with the EU as a whole, German "contributions [to military operations] have been heavily concentrated outside the purview of the UN, in missions deployed by NATO and the EU."[31] Germany's performance on the council has also attracted criticism. During the 2011 Libyan civil war, Germany's performance on the council has been described as "self-defeating" and downright "bad crisis management."[32]

India

India was a founding member of the UN, and it served its first term on the council in 1950 to 1951 (occupying the Commonwealth seat). After the enlargement of 1966, India served a further four times on the council as part of the Asia (now Asia-Pacific) group. In 1961, the leaders of India, Indonesia, Burma, Indonesia, Yugoslavia, Ghana, and Egypt founded the Non-Aligned Movement (NAM), a group that would play a central role in the UN throughout the Cold War. Of the G4 members, India is typically seen as possessing the strongest bid for a permanent seat. The Indian bid also has the strongest base of support in the General Assembly. India (Asia-Pacific) is the third largest troop contributor to UN peacekeeping, the tenth largest economy (likely to become the third largest by 2050), and the second most populous country.[33]

Although the Indian bid has found strong support among the membership at large, there are a number of serious considerations, which have been raised as potential roadblocks. Firstly, although Sino-Indian relations have improved over recent years, China "has no love for India."[34] A long running territorial dispute (over Aksai Chin and Arunachal Pradesh) remains alive. A short border war erupted in 1962, then again in 1967 and 1987 (as skirmishes). In spite of the outstanding dispute, China has stated its support for India's "aspiration to play a greater role in the United Nations."[35] Secondly, India and neighbor Pakistan have been embroiled in a long and complex conflict, which dates back to the foundation of both states and includes four major wars. The council deployed the UN Military Observer Group in India and Pakistan (UNMOGIP) to Kashmir and Jammu in 1949 to observe a ceasefire agreement. The mission remains to this day. If India became a permanent member, the role of the council as a potential Chapter VI arbiter in any future conflict would be profoundly compromised.

Thirdly, India has never signed the Nuclear Non-Proliferation Treaty (NPT).[36] In 1998, India's first nuclear test provoked US scorn and sanctions. At the time it was said that India had disqualified itself from consideration for a permanent seat. If India were to gain a permanent seat, the already shaky credibly of the council's actions on non-proliferation would be further undermined. The council would be seen to be enforcing a contradictory set of policies vis-à-vis Iran and North Korea. Fourthly, the positions adopted by India during its last term on the council (2011–2012) were not particularly well received by the US and some observers. One senior UN official even characterized India's performance as "not a good example of either leading or following."[37]

Brazil

During the deliberations at Dumbarton Oaks, the question of Brazilian permanent membership was discussed. Roosevelt was a champion for Brazil, as was his secretary of state, Cordell Hull. The other major powers saw five permanents in a council of 11. If a sixth were included, a new set of dilemmas would emerge, they argued. FDR was not dissuaded. Brazil was not a great power, but neither was the ROC or France (which had only a postwar provisional government at the time). Hull made the request for Brazil on the basis of "its [Brazil's] size, resources, and active participation in the war against Germany."[38] The British and the Russians were lukewarm on the proposals. Ultimately, the United States did not push the issue. As a consolation, the Latin American electoral group was afforded two elected seats, Brazil has been elected to serve on the Security Council the more than any other member of the UN. In its original format, Brazil served a total of four terms. After 1965, it served another six times, including three times since 1998. Brazil is seventh largest economy, the fifth most populous country, and is a regional power in Latin America. On the peacekeeping front, Brazil has been involved in UN missions deployed to the Portuguese-speaking countries of East Timor, Mozambique, and Angola. Brazilian peacekeepers have also played a role in Haiti and the Congo. As of January 2015, 1,693 Brazilian personnel were deployed to UN missions, which placed the country at nineteenth on the list of contributors. In financial terms, Brazil is the tenth largest financial contributor to the UN general budget (2.93 percent). While Brazil is a regional power it is situated in a predominately Spanish-speaking region. This concern was first voiced at Dumbarton Oaks: "the inclusion of Portuguese-speaking Brazil would fail to placate the other Latin American nations, which would probably ask that permanent representation also be granted to the much larger Spanish-speaking population."[39] Latin American opposition to Brazil's bid is spearheaded by Argentina. Other Latin American and Caribbean UfC members include Colombia, Costa Rica, and Mexico. On the other side of the ledger stands Chile and Guatemala, both of which support Brazil's bid. The United States has been uncomfortable about Brazil's involvement with the non-interventionist BRICS states (Brazil, Russia, India, China and South Africa). US discomfort peaked in 2011 during the Libya crisis. After Libya and Syria, the United States is clearly concerned about a potential polarization of the council between the West and the non-interventionist BRICS. The US is therefore unlikely to openly support the Brazilian bid.

Uniting for Consensus (UfC)

The UfC are opposed to new permanency, generally, and to the plans of the G4, specifcally. The group comprises a coalition of middle and smaller powers: Italy, Pakistan, Turkey, South Korea, Mexico, Colombia, Argentina, Malta, San Marino, Costa Rica, and Canada (Indonesia and China are also involved). It is believed that the UfC receives the support of between 20–30 members. The bloc is united in a common cause, but divided on motivation. There are those that have taken a principled stand; these members of the group "consider the very existence of permanent membership to be wrong, and they have no desire to compound the original sin by adding more members to a category they dislike."[40] The other members of the group are the regional rivals of the G4: Pakistan against India, Argentina against Brazil, and Italy against Germany. Although, these countries rhetorically draw on principle to justify their position in the UfC, the reality is that these countries are motivated principally by national interest.

The UfC have proposed a doubling of the number elected members, bringing the number to 20 and the council to a total of 25. Their plan was laid down in a draft resolution (A/59/L.68) prior to the Millennium+5 Summit:

> The Security Council shall consist of twenty-five Members of the United Nations...The General Assembly shall elect twenty other members of the United Nations to be non-permanent members of the Security Council, due regard being specially paid, in the first instance, to the contribution of Members of the United Nations to the maintenance of international peace and security and to the other purposes of the Organization, and also to equitable geographical distribution.[41]

The proposal also called for the allocation of the 20-elected seat using the following pattern: six for Africa, five for Asia, four for GRULAC, three for WEOG, and two for EEG. Canadian Permanent Representative Allan Rock suggested that the proposal would leave "it to the members of each regional group to decide which Member-states should sit in those seats, and for how long."[42] In 2009, Italy and Colombia moved another proposal, which they said was a "visible step forward from the group's 2005 proposal."[43] The plan, however, did not commit the group to a seat allocation or even a total seat number. It proposed the creation of an unspecified number of additional seats, in either a new longer-term category or regular two-year elected category. The plan gave two options regarding term limit for the longer-term seats:

- Option A would allow a regional seat holder to occupy the seat for between three and five years, without the possibility of renewal.
- Option B set a term limit of two-years with the possibility of two consecutive renewals (equal to six years).

Under the plan the regular two-year elected seats would be allocated to small states, medium sized states, Africa, Asia, GRULAC, and EEG. Yet, the introduction of medium and small states to electoral contests added an unhelpful new layer of complexity to the debate, as a host of definitional issues emerged, namely what constitutes a small or medium state? In the spring of 2015, the UfC issued a brief document clumsily titled UN Security Council Reform Is Possible: Compromise to Achieve Broad-Based Consensus Is Needed. Distribution of this new document raised the question: what was the UfC's actual position? The document itself provided little in the way of clarity. First, the UfC stated that it would "support a UNSC of up to 26 in total."[44] Second, the group would, through negotiations in the immediate term, seek to "address how to best limit the use of the veto in circumstances that include, but are not limited to, mass atrocities."[45] Third, reiterating its previous statements, the UfC continues to support the creation of long-term renewable elected seats, as well as an increase the number of regular elected seats.

Africa (C-10)

Although the African bloc openly espouses a common position, the continent is far from united on the issue. Some African countries are members of the C-10 (which conforms to the Ezulwini Consensus), while others are supporters or members of the L-69 (41 countries, including 11 from Africa) and the UfC. Both the Ezulwini Consensus and the Sirte Declaration call for two African permanent seats with veto power and five elected seats (an additional two seats). The African bloc has presented this position as a non-negotiable. The logic of the African position is quite straightforward: if the P-5 retain their veto, then the privilege should be extended to new permanent members.

Nigeria and South Africa are considered to be the most logical candidates for African permanent membership. As the preeminent members of the African bloc, both have pursued strategies to advantage their position vis-à-vis permanency. Both countries have looked to harmonize their position with the G4, which would involve shelving the demand for immediate veto extension. However, there has been stiff resistance to a softening of the common position. Rival countries and the principled alike have orchestrated resistance to a position convergent with that of the G4 or other blocs. Others in the bloc also insist on an accountability mechanism that would bind African permanent members to their region in some way.

The Committee of Ten Heads of State on United Nations Security Council Reform (C-10) coordinates the African position on behalf of the AU (53 countries at present, with Egypt suspended). In general terms, the C-10 believes that council reform should address "the historical injustice that left Africa the only continent not represented in the council's permanent membership, and under-represented in its non-permanent membership."[46] The African bloc has held off nominating their preferred permanent members. This creates a two-fold problem. Firstly, many states, including the US, will not openly support a position on new permanency that is embedded with such ambiguities. Secondly, rivalries between the various African aspirants inhibit African unity and intra-bloc convergence. The big five African powers—Egypt, Nigeria, Ethiopia, Algeria, and South Africa—have been touted as possible candidates for the two slated African permanent seats.

- **Egypt** is both an African and Arab regional power. It is the most populous country of North Africa (82 million) and is the forty-second largest economy in the world (based on nominal GDP). Egypt has the eighteenth most powerful military in the world and possesses the largest military on the continent (with almost 500,000 personnel).
- **Ethiopia** is the preeminent power in the Horn of Africa. It has long stood as a champion of Pan-Africanism[47] and now hosts the African Union Headquarters. Ethiopia is the second most populous country on the continent (90 million in 2015 and 185 million by 2050), and it boasts Africa's tenth largest economy and fourth most powerful military.
- **Nigeria** is the largest country in Africa, in terms of both population and economy. It is a country that has served more terms on the council than any other African member: five terms in all. According to projections, Nigeria will become the ninth largest economy and the fifth most populous country in the world by 2050. Nigeria's current power projection is compromised by the Boko Haram insurgency.
- **Algeria** is regional power in North Africa and the Maghreb. Although, it has a modest population and economy, Algeria is still considered one of the traditional middle powers of Africa. The country has been preoccupied with a regional Islamist insurgency and the Arab Spring, which has affected neighboring countries. Algeria is a military power, which boasts the highest level of military expenditure on the continent.
- **South Africa** is a regional power and has maintained significant influence throughout Africa since the end of apartheid. The country currently boasts the second largest economy in Africa and arguably the continent's most effective military. South African mediators have also been actively involved in ending conflicts in Burundi, Comoros, DRC, and Zimbabwe. In 2011, South Africa become the fifth member of the BRIC bloc (Brazil, Russia, India, China), now called BRICS (Brazil, Russia, India, China and South Africa).

As Africa holds 54 of the 129 votes required to adopt a charter amendment, which effectively gives the bloc kingmaker status in the General Assembly (the other kingmakers being the legislatures of the P-5).[48]

L-69

The L-69 takes its name from the draft resolution A/61/L.69 of 2007, which was an effort to move the membership toward text-based negotiations. The L-69 is a regional crosscutting bloc comprised of 40 developing states from Latin America, the Caribbean (CARICOM), and Africa. The membership also includes G4 aspirants India and Brazil, and African aspirants South Africa and Nigeria. In 2012, the L-69 drafted a resolution that outlined their preferred model. The model envisages a 27-seat council with six new permanent seats and six new elected seats. Included in the L-69 plan is the allocation of an elected seat for a small island state (SIS). 37 UN member-states form part of the Alliance of Small Island States (ASIS), which represents 20 percent of the total membership of the organization—another powerful bloc in the General Assembly.

L-69 believes that the veto should be abolished. However, the L-69 insists that, as the long as the veto exists, it should be extended to all new permanent members, in line with the African C-10 position. Interestingly, the L-69 and G4 submissions to the 2015 Framework Document appear remarkably similar in a number of key areas, including the number and distribution of permanent and elected seats. These similarities have raised a number of questions about the overlapping nature of its membership. All of the group's members are actually also members of other regional groups, including CARICOM (Caribbean Community), the Africa group, and the G4.

Table 3.5 L-69 proposed model

Groupings	Elected	New Permanent	Permanent
WEOG	2 (+0)	1	3
Asia-Pacific	2 (+1)	2	1
Africa	3 (+2)	2	–
Eastern Europe	1 (+1)	–	1
GRULAC	2 (+1)	1	–
Small Island States	0 (+1)	–	–
TOTAL	16	6	5

The Permanent Five

Russia, China, and the United States appear unlikely to dive headlong into the reform debate unless a compromise position is first found between the four key blocs (Africa, L-69, UfC, and the G4). The three predominant permanent members feel eminently comfortable with the status quo. Change, of any sort, would upset the balance of the council and would most likely result in a dilution of their power. Hence, there exists no compunction to alter the council, in spite of the calls for change. As Richard Gowan and Nora Gordon rightly suggest, the impulse for reform does not and will not reside with the P-5 (i.e. the top-down approach). Yet, at the same time, the P-5 must be readily amendable to any reform worked out by the membership at large.

France and the United Kingdom

In March 2010, France and the UK issued a joint statement on council reform. The statement offered support to the G4 position, while advocating for an intermediate solution aimed at ending the deadlocked negotiations. Such a solution would create a set of longer renewable term seats, which after a time could be made permanent. As of 2015, both countries had abandoned the intermediate solution. France continues to spearhead a campaign for a code of conduct regulating the veto in situations of mass atrocities or genocide.[49] The code of conduct has been discussed by the working methods reform group known as Accountability Coherence and Transparency (ACT), and is also strongly supported by civil society organizations including the Elders (see below). By early 2015, France and the United Kingdom's united front had begun to break down. France signaled that it was open to entertaining the prospect of an extension of veto rights to new permanent members, while the UK retained its stance against the extension of veto rights.

China

In official statements, Chinese representatives have issued rather ambiguous statements regarding reform. Two Chinese positions, however, are very clear. Firstly, like the Russia and the United States, China does not support reforms that tamper with the privilege of veto. Secondly, China is bitterly opposed to the Japanese bid. China's stated position is that, "priority should be given to increasing the representation of developing countries, in particular African countries."[50] In the reform debate, Africa is China's primarily focus; it will not lend its "support to a reform proposal that fails to win widespread support across the African continent."[51] However, Chinese support for Africa does not imply support for the African common position. Theoretically China should be sympathetic to the cause of fellow BRICS members Brazil, India, and South Africa. However, the addition of the G4 countries as permanent members would not necessarily suit its interests. Interestingly China is also nominally associated with the UfC and acted in concert with the Arab group and the UfC to reject Rattray's clean-slate framework approach to negotiations. It appears that the middle-power grouping of the UfC "plays to China's advantage."[52]

Russia

Russia has been both unyielding and flexible on certain aspects of reform. The Russians are seemingly unwilling to enter into a conversation on any veto, arguing that it should continue to represent, "an important instrument that encourages Security Council members to search for balanced solutions."[53] Russia simply will not allow the veto to be abolished, altered, or extended to new permanent members. Russia also has made statements that make clear its preference on three matters. Firstly, in the past, Russia has marked Japan, Germany, India, Brazil, South Africa, and Egypt for permanent membership, which translates as tacit support for the G4 position. It could be assumed that the Russians view the inclusion of BRICS aspirants as an exercise in bloc creation—a counterweight to the Western permanent members and their aspirants Germany and Japan. In practice, BRICS alignment cannot necessarily be guaranteed. Secondly, Russian representatives have continued to call for a compact body whose number should not exceed the low 20s, preferably 20. The concept of a small council is tied to the matter of efficiency; a body that is too large becomes unwieldy. Thirdly, even though the procedures of the General Assembly would require a two-thirds majority, for Russia nothing short of consensus in the General Assembly will be necessary to ensure harmony.

United States

The US is "open to modest Council expansion in permanent and non-permanent membership."[54] Like Russia, the US has always been sceptical of enlargement exceeding the low-20s (i.e. the addition of more than half a dozen new members). Gowan and Gordon have noted that "the US, China, and Russia appear sceptical [about reform], with U.S. interest declining since the matter received some attention in 2009–2010."[55]

The relative decline in the Washington's appetite for a meaningfully discussion is undoubtedly linked to the polarization of the council over Syria and Libya. In Washington, an attitudinal shift towards India and Brazil occurred following the events surrounding the adoption of resolution 1973 (on Libya). For the US, any proposed reform must meet the following criterion:

- Enlargement must preserve or enhance council effectiveness and efficiency;
- Candidate Permanent members must be known in advance;
- New permanency should be based, not on geography or size, but on a candidate country's willingness to commit to the maintenance of peace and security;
- No change in the structure of the veto;

Reform must be negotiated through the legislative processes on the hill, where a potentially hostile senate could theoretically scuttle any changes to the UN charter, as it did with Wilson's plans to join the League of Nations.[56]

In summarizing the positions of the P-5 several commonalities emerge. Firstly, the P-5 does not favor the dilution or abolition of their veto privileges, or the extension of that privilege to any new permanent member. Secondly, the P-5 generally favors a compact body of around 21 seats. Both Russia and US have repeatedly signaled their preference for a compact council to insure against rampant inefficiency.

Civil society proposals

For the most part, the debate on Security Council reform is confined to the New York diplomatic set. Few interventions from outside this New York conversation can be noted. Even within the vast civil society community in New York, engagement on the issue has been lax. The problem is amplified further afield in the capitals of the world. Only a few think tanks and NGOs have sought to change the conversation at home or abroad. More recent activity is mildly encouraging, however.

The Elders

In early 2015, the Elders, a group of eminent thought leaders and elder states people (including Kofi Annan, Jimmy Carter, Martii Ahtisaari, Mary Robinson, and Lakhdar Brahimi), issued a statement entitled "A UN Fit for Purpose." The statement included four recommendations, calling for (1) veto restraint, (2) new category of Security Council membership, (3) a stronger voice for civil society through the Arria formula, and (4) a more independent secretary-general.

Veto restraint is not an original idea. It is a centerpiece of a French initiative launched in 2013 and forms part of the S-5/ACT proposals and even Razali's plan. The Elders call on the P-5 to "pledge themselves to greater and more persistent effort to find common ground, especially in crises where populations are being subjected to, or threatened with, genocide or other atrocity crimes."[57] The pledge would informally bind the P-5 to a commitment "not to use, or threaten to use, their veto in such crises without explaining, clearly and in public, what alternative course of action they propose."[58]

The new category of membership, proposed by the Elders, is essentially an endorsement of the concept of renewability. The Elders suggest that, "instead of new permanent members" a new cateory of longer-term renewable membership should be created.[59] The suggestion is marketed as a compromise solution, which allows aspirant countries the opportunity to serve as de-facto permanent members, but only if they continue to "enjoy the confidence of other member-states."[60]

Elect the Council

In 2015, the Institute for Security Studies (ISS) based in South Africa launched a civil society campaign calling for a more radical overhaul of the council's structure. The campaign takes a fundamentally different approach to the issue by seeking to first build to global partnership of civil society organizations—creating a groundswell—before engaging governments. The model proposes a 24-member council operating under a proportional representation formula. Eight members would occupy five-year seats (renewable), while 16 members would occupy three-year seats (non-renewable). Under the proposed model, members would be elected to the council on the basis of their contribution to the maintenance of international peace and security.

In terms of the allocation of seats by region, Elect the Council calls for an almost complete overhaul. EEG and WEOG are each allocated one five-year seat and two three-years seats, while the Asia-Pacific, Africa, and GRULAC electoral groupings would each receive two five-year seats and four three year seats. The most radical element of the proposal is the abolition of the veto. A 15-year period of transition has been proposed to allow for the incremental normalization of the status of the P-5. At year one, the P-5 would be stripped of their current veto privileges, but they would be granted weighted voting rights. The transitory weighted voting system would only operate for 10 years from the commencement of the proposed arrangements. For an initial five-year period (years one to five), a permanent member's vote would carry the weight of three votes. During the subsequent five-year period (years six to 10), the weight of a permanent member's vote would be reduced to two. After the 15-year period of transition the P5 would "contest for elections in their respective regions should they wish to remain on the UNSC."[61] At such time, all members of the council would each possess one vote, with decisions being carried by a two-thirds majority.

Conclusion

The history of council reform can be summarized, as a collection of plans, processes, consensuses, and negotiations to nowhere. After 20 years of debate, the composition of the council remains unaltered. The blocs have abjectly failed to negotiate in good faith. Instead, they have put forward self-serving, take it or leave it plans; and then proceeded to lock horns to the point of stalemate. As such, the real negotiations have yet to begin.

Notes

1 Robert C. Hilderbrand, *Dumbarton Oaks: The Origins of the United Nations and the Search for Postwar Security* (Chapel Hill: University of North Carolina Press, 1990), 122.
2 Hilderbrand, *Dumbarton Oaks*, 128.
3 Hilderbrand, *Dumbarton Oaks*, 128.
4 Hilderbrand, *Dumbarton Oaks*, 128.
5 UN Charter, Chapter V, Article 27 (3).
6 General Assembly resolution 1991 A, 17 December 1963.
7 Dimitris Bourantonis, *The History and Politics of UN Security Council Reform* (Abingdon: Routledge, 2005), 28.
8 UN Charter, Chapter XVIII, Article 108.
9 General Assembly resolution 55/2. *United Nations Milennium Declaration* (A/55/L.2), 8 September 2000, para. 30.
10 High-Level Panel on Threats Challenges and Change, *A More Secure World: Our Shared Responsibility* (New York: United Nations, 2014), 109.
11 Kofi Annan, *In Larger Freedom: Towards Development, Security and Human Rights for All* (New York: United Nations, 2004), 61.
12 Edward C. Luck, "How Not to Reform the United Nations," *Global Governance: A Review of Multilateralism and International Organizations* 11 (2005), 407–414.
13 Luck, "How Not to Reform the United Nations."
14 The substance of the resolution covered six broad themes: (1) expansion in both permanent and non-permanent categories; (2) greater representation of the developing countries, including island and small States; (3) representation

of the developed countries and those with transition economies reflective of contemporary world realities; (4) comprehensive improvement in the working methods of the Security Council; (5) equitable geographical distribution; and (6) provision for a review.

15 Chair of the Inter-governmental Negotiations, *Non-Paper*, 2013. http://www.un.org/en/ga/president/68/pdf/letters/12102013Security_Council_Reform_Informals-10_December_2013.pdf.

16 *Report of the Open-ended Working Group on the Question of Equitable Representation on and Increase in the Membership of the Security Council and Other Matters related to the Security Council* (General Assembly A/62/47), 2008, 9

17 *Letter Dated 25 July 2012, from the Chair of the Intergovernmental Negotiations on the question of equitable representation on and increase in the membership of the Security Council and related matters,* 25 July 2012

18 *Letter Dated 13 May 2015, from the Permanent Representative of Jamaica addressed to the President of the General Assembly,* 13 May 2015.

19 General Assembly (A/69/L.92), 11 September 2015, 2.

20 General Assembly (A/69/L.92), 11 September 2015, 2.

21 General Assembly, *General Assembly Adopts, without Vote, "Landmark" Decision on Advancing Efforts to Reform, Increase Membership of Security Council*, 2015. http://www.un.org/press/en/2015/ga11679.doc.htm

22 General Assembly, *General Assembly Adopts, without Vote, "Landmark" Decision on Advancing Efforts to Reform, Increase Membership of Security Council*, 2015.

23 UN Charter, Chapter V, Article 23 (1).

24 *Report of the Open-ended Working Group on the Question of Equitable Representation on and Increase in the Membership of the Security Council and Other Matters related to the Security Council* (General Assembly A/62/47), 2008, 10.

25 Japan's membership application was vetoed by the USSR in 1952 and 1955.

26 The Constitution of Japan, Article 9.

27 Haruhiro Fukui, "Japan," in *National Security Cultures: Patterns of Global Governance*, ed. Emil J. Kirchner and James Sperling (Abingdon: Routledge, 2010), 260.

28 As of February 2015, Japan was ranked 52th on the list of troop contributors with a total of 272 personnel deployed to UNMISS.

29 Kyodo, "Article 9 a UNSC-bid hurdle: Powell," *Japan Times*, 14 August 2004. http://www.japantimes.co.jp/news/2004/08/14/national/article-9-a-unsc-bid-hurdle-powell/.

30 It's possible, with two elected WEOG seats, two elected Eastern Europe seats (11 of the group's 23 members are also EU members), Germany, France, and the UK.

31 Kai Michael Kenkel, "Peacekeeping Contributor Profile: Germany," *Providing for Peacekeeping*, 3 April 2014 http://www.providingforpeacekeeping.org/2014/04/03/contributor-profile-germany/.

32 Richard Gowan, *Australia in the Security Council* (Sydney: Lowy Institute for International Policy, 2014), 7.

33 Akhilesh Pillalamarri, "China Should Back India for a Permanent UN Security Council Seat," *The Diplomat*, February 2015. http://thediplomat.

com/2015/02/china-should-back-india-for-a-permanent-un-security-council-seat/

34 Richard Wilcox, "America Should Insist: Yes, a Security Council Seat for India," *New York Times*, 10 February 2003. http://www.nytimes.com/2003/02/10/opinion/10iht-edwilcox_ed3_.html.

35 Atul Aneja, "China 'respects' India's U.N. Seat Bid," *The Hindu*, 13 February 2015. http://www.thehindu.com/news/international/world/china-respects-indias-un-seat-bid/article6888674.ece.

36 Wilcox, "America Should Insist: Yes, a Security Council Seat for India."

37 Anonymous Interviewee, Interview with Author, July 2011.

38 Hilderbrand, *Dumbarton Oaks*.

39 Hilderbrand, *Dumbarton Oaks*, 125.

40 Shashi Tharoor, "Security Council Reform: Past, Present, and Future," *Ethics & International Affairs* 25 (2011): para. 9.

41 *Reform of the Security Council* (General Assembly A/59/L.68), 21 July 2005.

42 Statement by Allan Rock (Canada) to the General Assembly (GA/10371), 26 July 2005.

43 *Agenda Item 119: Question of Equitable Representation on and Increase in the Membership of the Security Council and Other Related Matters* (General Assembly A/64/CRP.1), 21 January 2010.

44 Uniting for Consensus, *UN Security Council Reform is Possible*, 2015. http://centerforunreform.org/sites/default/files/UfC%20Doc%202015.pdf#overlay-context=.

45 Uniting for Consensus, *UN Security Council Reform is Possible*, 2015.

46 General Assembly, *Speakers, Voicing Frustration at Lack of Progress, Call for Security Council Reforms to Reflect Current Political Realities*, 2014. http://www.un.org/press/en/2014/ga11583.doc.htm.

47 Ethiopia strongly resisted Italian colonialism in the late 1800s and founded the NAM and the OAU.

48 Although, this is based on the assumption that Africa would vote as one on Council reform, which should not be taken as a given.

49 Salil Shetty, "Unshackle the United Nations," *New York Times*, 25 February 2015. http://www.nytimes.com/2015/02/25/opinion/unshackle-the-united-nations.html.

50 Statement by Liu Jieyi (China) to the 68th Session of the General Assembly (GA/11450), 7 November 2013.

51 Xue Lei, *China as a Permanent Member of the United Nations Security Council* (New York: Friedrich-Ebert-Stiftung, 2014), 14.

52 Bruce Gilley, "China's Discovery of Middle Powers," in *Middle Powers and the Rise of China*, eds. Bruce Gilley & Andrew O'Neil (Washington, DC: Georgetown University Press, 2014), 54.

53 Sputnik International, "Russia Ready to Consider "Rational" Security Council Reform," *Sputnik News*, 16 November 2012. http://sputniknews.com/world/20121116/177502747.html.

54 Statement by Ann Elizabeth Jones (United States) to the 69th Session of the General Assembly (GA/11583), 12 November 2014.

55 Richard Gowan and Nora Gordon, *Pathways to Security Council Reform* (New York: New York University Center on International Cooperation, May 2014), 5.

56 A two-thirds supermajority of the US Senate is required (or 67 of 100).
57 Statement by the Elders, *Strengthening the United Nations*, 7 February 2015. http://theelders.org/sites/default/files/2015-04-22_elders-statement-strengtheni ng-the-un.pdf.
58 Statement by the Elders, *Strengthening the United Nations*.
59 Statement by the Elders, *Strengthening the United Nations*.
60 Statement by the Elders, *Strengthening the United Nations*.
61 Elect the Council, *Elect the Council Motivation and Proposals* (version 3), 2015. http://www.electthecouncil.org/documents/ElecttheCouncil.v3.pdf.

4 An expanded council

- **Representativeness**
- **Power and power projection**
- **Democratization and inclusion**
- **Efficiency, unanimity and "lowest common denominator-ism"**
- **Contribution to the maintenance of international peace and security**
- **Conclusion**

Reform is aimed at improving performance, altering something for the better. It is concerned with repairing defects and overcoming limitations in order to realize some higher state of performance or effectiveness.[1] Reform is about evolution, not revolution, as it seeks to eliminate the faults of a system without fundamentally altering the system itself. Reform should seek to improve the council through enhancing its capacity to undertake its important work. The model of agency, presented in the preceding chapter, provides a potential schema for reform: markedly enhancing the council's agency should constitute the aim of any reform. The identification of the key determinants of council agency draws into sharper focus the key determinants for reform—as they are essentially one in the same.

Throughout the next series of chapters, the tenets of council agency will be routinely invoked. They will be used to probe the claims of would-be reformists. This chapter will subject the claims of the proponents of new permanency to scrutiny. It cautions against accepting the rather unsophisticated arguments presented by these proponents. The framework for the chapter relies on a number of oft-recited concepts such as representativeness, diversity, efficiency, democratization, and equality.

Representativeness

The concept of representativeness is perhaps the most frequently used term in the debate on reform. Representativeness, broadly speaking, is concerned with the notion that an executive decision-making institution should accurately reflect the collective will and interests of the whole. Talk of representativeness begs the question: representative of what, of whom? Is a council member beholden to the interests of its electoral group? Or are members simply indicative of the typical (a symbol of the broader group)? The difference is more than semantic.

The first and stronger mode of representativeness is something akin to representative democracy, whereby a member of a constituency is chosen by that constituency to represent its interests in a parliament or legislature. Through the process of being elected to serve in the parliament, the elected is representative of the electors (i.e. the voters). In theory, the parliament should mirror the electorate. In this system, representatives are held accountable to their constituents by way of regular elections. Best practice dictates that representatives hold regular consultations with their constituents to sound out public opinion and reorder their priorities. The second and weaker mode of representativeness is akin to representative sampling. Under this mode, a representative is a mere sample of a wider group. The sample should be an accurate reflection of this wider population; otherwise it would not be representative. There are no inferences beyond this. Hence, the representative is not accountable to the wider group and cannot be said to represent the interests of the wider group. The UN operates under the second, weaker definition. Representativeness does not operate on a single dimension. Nor do all member-states hold to a common definition of the term. Reformists of various persuasions have come to define representation in terms of relative power, geography, and perspectives on international order.

Geopolitical realities of the twenty-first century

The relative power of states (geography, population, economy, resources, military, diplomacy, and national identity) is one particular rendering or dimension on which representation might rest. For many, the council's permanent seats should be reserved only for the great or emerging powers of the world. Definitions of power vary, however. A list of great powers might include the big three of the EU (Germany, France, and the UK), Japan, India, China, Russia, and the United States, while a list of the emerging or potential great powers might include Indonesia, Mexico, Turkey, Nigeria, South Africa, South Korea, and Egypt.

The geopolitical realities argument centers on what Stephen Walt has termed the "absurdity"[2] of the antiquated composition of present council—a council without India, Brazil, Japan, Germany, and select

African powers. According to Walt, the council should seek to become more representative of the realities of the twenty-first century. The present council is reflective of the world as it was in 1945 and should be updated to reflect the new centers of gravity of the twenty-first century. In recent years, new centers of power located in Beijing, Brasília, and New Delhi have emerged. The campaign for new permanency is an effort aimed at formally recognizing these new centers of power in the UN system. It is argued that the proposed enlargement will transform the legitimacy of the council by balancing the permanent ledger. Currently, four of the permanent members belong to the OECD (Organisation for Economic Cooperation and Development) or the global north, while China is the solitary member from the global south. The G4's more balanced P-11 would include six powers of the global north (Japan, Germany, Russia, the UK, the United States, and France) and five of the global south (China, India, Brazil, and two African powers).

Former Secretary-General Kofi Annan has articulated the potential threat posed by the status quo ad infinitum: "if the Security Council does not reform, but expects its decisions to be accepted and adopted by emerging powers, they have something else coming."[3] In this statement, Annan draws a link between the fulfillment of self-interest and legitimacy, suggesting that emerging powers will not comply with council edicts unless they are granted permanency. In other words, "formal presence in a decision making body may lead a state to support its decisions more than it would if it had not been present."[4] According to this argument, legitimation is the "project of having one's self-interest satisfied."[5] To use an example: if Japan were to become a permanent member of the council, its self-interest would be served. As a consequence of receiving a permanent seat, Japan would likely come to view the council and its decisions as legitimate.

Annan has also suggested that the inclusion of emerging powers (India, Indonesia, Brazil, Nigeria and South Africa) would curb the use of the veto. He argues that, in a new council (inclusive of emerging powers), if a permanent member were to exercise its veto, in defiance of overwhelming majority of members, it would be "taking on the rest of the world, not only in abstract,"[6] but in the very presence of the emerging powers. Annan's theory is based on the assumption that the emerging powers would act to modify the behavior of the permanent membership, and thus moderate the veto. Then again, the move might actually work in reverse—to embolden the veto-wielding P-5. The more likely scenario is an amplified polarization between the interventionist and the non-interventionist powers on the council.

Firstly, anointing a new cadre of the most militarily and economically powerful may feed into already existing perceptions of elitism. Currently the council is viewed by many member-states as an elite, self-selected club of the world's powerful. Inviting new powerful members to join the club does not change the fact that it is still a club of the powerful. In all likelihood, the small and medium states would continue to hold to this perception. A "happy few"[7] would be content with the outcome, while an unhappy majority would remain marginalized.

Secondly, recognizing the geopolitical realities of the early twenty-first century, and then cementing these realities into place, may make it more difficult for the UN to recognize the geopolitical realities of the mid and late twenty-first century. In short, new permanency will not future-proof the council. Soon enough a new host of members will rally for recognition. For instance, by 2050, Indonesia will rank as the fifth largest country in terms of population, and will boast perhaps the fourth largest economy. It is also projected that South Korea, by 2030, will be the eighth largest economy (above France and Russia), and even today possesses the eighth most capable military in the world. Similarly, both Mexico and Turkey will continue to rank among the top 20 economies. Profound shifts in comparative national power will continue to occur over the course of the coming decades. Static reforms that neglect this issue are simply creating problems for the would-be reformers of the future. Moreover, any future expansion to accommodate new permanent members would add to the inefficiencies inherent to a larger council.

Thirdly, it would be prudent to pose the question: How long will India, Brazil and China continue to represent the global south? On the human development index, a country such as Brazil is classified as highly developed, while India, Nigeria, and South Africa are all placed in the medium development category. Both Japan and Germany belong to the very highly developed global north. Their ascension to the council would add two advanced economies of the global north to the three incumbents—France, the United Kingdom, and the United States.

Finally, it is questionable as to whether recognizing the geopolitical realities of the twenty-first century, through the institutionalization of new permanency, would deliver the performance gains mooted. The council would be empowered through marginal legitimacy gains, as identified above. However, this says nothing of the other elements of council agency. Are the aspirants prepared to devote themselves to generating and implementing resolutions? Are they prepared to provide the necessary leadership and political will to carry forward council interventions? Are they prepared to furnish the requisite resources to support the implementation of council decisions?

Perspectives on international order

Another school of thought frames representation using the partitions of culture, history, and national perspective. Ramesh Thakur explained the nature of this form of representation in the report, "What is Equitable Geographic Representation in the Twenty-first Century," stating that "if cultures, civilizations and religions represent the most salient cleavage in contemporary affairs, then, even if they do not necessarily lead to an inexorable clash based on an immutable conflict of interests, they might still need to be recognized formally in the world's preeminent international organization."[8]

What should the council be doing and what should it not be doing? These questions and their answers frame the debate on UN order. Clearly, member-states with different strategic cultures have come to view the UN in wildly differing ways. The notion of strategic culture is particularly instructive. A member-states perspective vis-à-vis the UN is informed by its strategic culture. Many member-states of the global south have come to view the a more activist council as the "cloak of a new form of imperialism"[9]—a council dominated, in part, by neo-colonialist hegemons intent on shaping the UN order to suit their interests.

Since the late 1980s, the UN, through the Security Council, has become a more interventionist institution, quantitatively and qualitatively. The council's remit has been gradually redefined to include a range of non-traditional threats such as internal conflict, coup d'états, humanitarian crises, terrorism, and epidemics. A more activist group of largely Western states (the global north) has driven the new agenda. Another group hold firm to the non-interventionist cause of Article 2 (7), uncomfortable with invasive interventions authorized under Chapter VII.

The English school of international relations theorizes that two branches—pluralism and solidarism—can be used to explain the difference: "pluralism is concerned solely with the minimum goal of inter-state co-existence, whereas solidarism is concerned with the higher goal of the welfare of individual human persons living in separate states."[10] Solidarism is the natural father of the contemporary council and its expanded remit. Concepts such as the Responsibility to Protect (RtoP) are also born of the solidarist or post-Westphalian traditions. Pluralism is a different school of thought that relies on the insistence that there is no possibility of a solidarist world society (universal normative vision) because of state-based identity (nationalism) and differing conceptions of what constitutes the good life. Security, for pluralists, is based on the system of mutual recognition of sovereignty, which positions the state as both the agent and referent of security. The pluralist conception of the UN order prioritizes sovereignty.

Is the goal of reform to have "inside the Council as full a sample of possible views in the General Assembly"?[11] The inclusion of post-colonial states on the council would balance the contest, and allow for a truer representation of the values and views on the floor of the General Assembly. Should the council be reflective of the diversity of the world of states? If so, what definition of diversity should be used? But does diversity markedly enhance the council's agency? The membership must address these questions in order to come to terms with the potential polarizing dynamics of a new council. The different and potentially incompatible strategic cultures of the aspirant powers make unity of purpose improbable. Polarization and disunity, on the other hand, gives targeted parties an opportunity to divide and conquer the council.

Equitable geographical representation

Each country carries a unique historically and geographically informed perspective on matters of foreign and strategic policy. In fact, at the UN, each member-state is singular and sovereign. Although member-states are influenced by their membership of electoral groupings, regional organizations, and alliance structures, they rarely, if ever, claim to represent these groupings within the UN system. Member-states are representative of their own position, first and foremost. For instance, if elected to the council, New Zealand would serve as a representative of a small island state, rather than an agent of the Small Island States (SISs) grouping. It is plausible that New Zealand would serve the interests of the broader cohort of smaller island states in certain matters, but one should not discount the prerogatives of national interest, which can work to erode a country's loyalties to electoral groupings. The regionalization argument appears workable when applied to regional arrangements or security communities that are maintained by countries with close working relationships—highly socialized settings like the EU, for instance. It becomes more difficult an argument to sustain when such an approach is applied to regions beset by long standing rivalries. In all but a few regions, the latter is the case: is India representative of South Asia or Brazil representative of Latin America or Japan for East Asia? In South Asia, India and Pakistan are nuclear rivals and continue to contest the Kashmir frontier. In East Asia, Japan has strong trading relations with its neighbors, but legacies of the Second World War continue to sour relations with

China and the Koreas. In Latin America, the relations are eminently more friendly, yet Portuguese-speaking Brazil still has a rival in Spanish-speaking neighbor Argentina.

Even if regional representation was a workable proposition, such a system of representation would be fraught with difficulty, not the least of which would be the negotiation of intricate intraregional decision-making processes that formulate common foreign policy. Even the most highly developed regional entity, the EU, which holds to a Common Security and Defence Policy (CSDP), is not immune to ongoing policy debates between its members. Furthermore, if common seats were sought, a charter amendment (Article 4) would be required to allow regional entities to officially join the organization.

The UN has always used the classification of macro-geographical regions as a standard framework for representation. The five current electoral group are organized geographically, albeit broadly defined. The Asia-Pacific group, comprising around a quarter of the membership (53/193), is an eclectic mix of countries that includes the likes of Jordan (in the Middle East), Japan (in North Asia), Kazakhstan (in Central Asia), Sri Lanka (in South Asia), Indonesia (in Southeast Asia), and Tonga (in the Pacific Islands). The Western European and Other (WEOG) group is geographically defined, in the first instance, and culturally defined, in the second. The group includes all Western European member-states, as well as four outliers—Australia, New Zealand, Canada (members of the Commonwealth electoral group prior to 1966), and Israel. Unless the geographic organization principle is abandoned, member-states will continue to nominally represent their regional electoral group.

In 1945, an original council of 11 represented a General Assembly of 51 (one to five). Today, a council of fifteen represents an assembly of 193 (one to 12). A council of 25 would hold a representation ratio of one to eight. In terms of geographical balance, the council is currently weighted towards WEOG, with three permanent members and two elected members. WEOG would remain overrepresented in an expanded council. However, proportional representation ratios would improve for both Asia, and Africa, while balance would be achieved with GRULAC and Eastern Europe. The following is a proportional representation profile of the five electoral groups.

- **WEOG:** The Western Europe and other group, under the current configuration, boasts three permanent seats—the United States (observer), the United Kingdom, and France—and two elected seats. The group comprises 15 percent (29/193) of the total membership of the General Assembly. In the council, WEOG holds three of the five vetoes and two of the ten elected seats—or 33.3 percent (5/15) of the total membership of the council. Under an expanded council, WEOG would be granted an extra permanent seat for Germany, while retaining its three original permanent seats and two elected seats. It would still remain grossly overrepresented at 24 percent to 15 percent.

- **GRULAC:** The Latin America and the Caribbean group is granted two elected seats under the current formula. With a total of 33 members (17 percent of the General Assembly), the group is currently underrepresented in the council (13.3 percent of the council) and is without a permanent seat. Under the G4 plan, GRULAC would be granted one permanent seat—Brazil—and an additional two elected seats, bringing the groups seat count to five. The group would be the only group to move from underrepresented to overrepresented at 20 percent (5/25) to 17 percent (33/193).

- **Eastern Europe:** In the current council, the Eastern European group holds one permanent seat—Russia—and one elected seat. The group is the smallest electoral group, with a total membership of 23 or 11.9 percent of the General Assembly. It therefore only marginally overrepresented on the council at 13.3 percent to 11.9 percent. Under the G4's proposed formula, the group would gain an extra elected seat, which would give the group a proportional balance in the council at 12 percent (3/15) to 11.9 percent (23/193).

- **Africa:** Under the current 15-seat composition, the African electoral group, with its 54 members, occupies three seats. The group is the largest electoral bloc (28 percent) in the General Assembly, but is grossly underrepresented on the Security Council, with 20 percent of total council membership and no permanent seat. Under the G4 formula, the African group would be granted two permanent seats and four elected seats, bringing the total African seat count to six in a 25-seat council. Africa would improve its position, but would still remain underrepresented at 24 percent to 28 percent.

- **Asia-Pacific:** Under the current composition, the Asia-Pacific group, an electoral group of 53 members, holds one permanent seat—China—and two elected seats. The Asia-Pacific group (53/193) comprises 27.5 percent of the total membership of the General Assembly and 20 percent (3/15) of the seats on the Security Council. Hence, the group is proportionally underrepresented on the council. Under the proposed G4 proposal, the group would hold three permanent seats—China, India, and Japan—and a further three elected seats. The group would continue to be promotionally underrepresented in the council, but only marginally, at 24 percent to 27.5 percent.

Power and power projection

The fourth argument follows that by granting permanency to those that are currently powerful, the council's agency and authority will be markedly enhanced. In simple terms, including the powerful on the council will make it more powerful.

Power

The council was founded the idea that the strong "adult nations" would act in concert to impose on their collective will on the "minor children" and the untrustworthy.[12] Together the powerful concert of four (later five) would police the world and enforce disarmament. The naïve assumption of the "un-selfish service"[13] of the great powers, coupled with a paternalistic vision of an interventionist cadre of policemen, undermined the practical functioning of the council. Sir Brian Urquhart explains the system and its logic:

> It was a pragmatic system based on the primacy of the strong—a "trusteeship of the powerful," as he then called it, or, as he put it later, "the Four Policemen." The concept was, as Vandenberg noted in his diary in April 1944, "anything but a wild-eyed internationalist dream of a world state. ... It is based virtually on a four-power alliance." Eventually this proved to be both the potential strength and the actual weakness of the future UN, an organization theoretically based on a concert of great powers whose own mutual hostility, as it turned out, was itself the greatest potential threat to world peace.[14]

Without the presence of the great powers, the council would almost be devoid of manifest influence. Each of the permanent members exerts considerable influence outside the domain of the council. When acting in concert, through the council, the P-5 bid to exercise their collective influence. In this way, the council can be viewed as a receptacle for the collective influence of the five. The calculations of states are clearly shaped by the council, when the permanent membership chooses to act in unity. A diplomatic signal sent via a Chapter VII resolution may only constitute words on paper, but these words are potentially backed by war, force of arms, the threat of force, or the threat or imposition of economic sanctions. The council's power is prefaced, in part, on its readiness to use force in the event of non-compliance. The case of Libya in 2011 is one such example. For Muammar Gaddafi, a failure to comply with the demands of the council for "an immediate end to the violence and calls for steps to fulfil the legitimate demands of the population"[15] led to the imposition of a no-fly zone and the authorization of the use of force. In the first instance, the council's demands were backed by sanctions and an ICC referral (resolution 1970), and then later by the use of force (resolution 1973). In this case, Gaddafi underestimated the resolve of council.

If the council displays a reticence to follow through on threats, then its influence is weakened. In this regard, resolve or timidity are directly linked to the unity of the permanent membership. In the case of Darfur, China possessed the greatest capacity to leverage the Government of Sudan (GoS), because the Chinese government maintained a variety of commercial interests in the country. Nevertheless, there was an unwillingness on the part of the Chinese to assert council positions. Instead, China primarily and Russia secondarily, acted to water-down resolutions, softening their language. This undermined the credibly of sanctions threats. Chinese and Russian abstentions were registered in relation to all key resolutions on Darfur (resolutions 1556, 1564, 1591, 1593, 1672 and 1706), with two exceptions (resolutions 1679 and 1769). This signaled to the GoS the Chinese and Russian opposition to three key instruments: (1) the imposition of sanctions, (3) the strengthening and widening of the arms embargo, (3) and the deployment of the UN Mission in South Sudan (UNMISS) without its consent. Moreover, when the panel of experts provided a list of 17 individuals recommended for targeted sanctions, China and Russia were able to trim the list down to only four names.[16] The council lacked unity, and therefore lacked assertiveness in the face of GoS's contempt and non-compliance. Instead, the council prevaricated, unable to accrue sufficient leverage or exercise what leverage it was able to accrue.

If a new set of powerful states are added to the permanent group of states, then surely the council's power to influence events and outcomes would be positively affected? In theory, the council should be empowered by the presence of great powers and regional powers alike. Regional powers exercise a claim to special privileges within their respective spheres of influence. In many crisis situations, regional powers possess many of the key ingredients the council requires: the will, capacity, and influence. Firstly, regional powers should, theoretically, act in their interests to preserve or restore regional security. It could be hypothesized that permanent membership might encourage leadership vis-à-vis specific regional files. Secondly, regional powers have special relations with their neighbors—the influence of proximity. Thirdly, each regional power maintains the capacity to undertake small-scale military efforts in the service of regional stability.

The line between leader and hegemon is thin, however. The danger of new permanency is that it reinforces and even formalizes regional spheres of influence, and strengthens the hegemonic claims of the powerful to the determinant of so-called subordinate smaller powers and their interests. Even without the veto, the dangers of new permanency manifest in a number of ways. Permanency could generate a "sense of superiority"[17] and a validation of entitled behavior among the newly anointed cadre. The worst-case scenario is that new permanency might inflame already existing regional tensions or create new ones. Most concerning is the potential for permanency to complicate and hinder council consideration of situations within the spheres of influence of the new permanent members. History has shown that, typically, most regional powers "seek to prevent external intrusions within their proximity."[18] Relying on this logic, it can be argued that regional powers may attempt to block or stymie council action.

Power projection

A secondary argument emerges from the discussion of power in the council. This secondary claim might be termed the heavy lifters argument: the countries possessing the greatest capacity for power projection can aid the council with the implementation of its resolutions. But what is power projection? And why might it be important for the council? Power projection is defined by the US Department of Defense as the "ability of a nation to apply all or some of its elements of national power—political, economic, informational, or military—to rapidly and effectively deploy and sustain forces in and from multiple dispersed locations to respond to crises, to contribute to deterrence, and to enhance regional stability."[19] In global terms, few of the aspirant members possess over-the-beach capacity, a blue-water navy, and commensurate forward air power capabilities; on almost all fronts, the P-5 continue to possess and project superior military power. Many middle powers also project military force, albeit on a regional level. In Asia, for instance, many non-aspirant countries such as South Korea, Turkey, and Indonesia retain, and continue to build, credible force projection capabilities.

Is power projection important for council decision-making? Would the granting of permanency to the countries that currently possess the greatest capacity for power projection make for a more capable council? The capabilities of the permanent membership have a direct and positive bearing on the council's influence in the world. As originally conceived, the overwhelming military and economic superiority of the P-5 was to be placed at the disposal of the council. Churchill even suggested that no country would dare challenge the postwar order through fear of a council backed by the might of the P-5. In 1990, Saddam Hussein was subject to the power of a permanent membership prepared to fully commit to the implementation of a Chapter VII resolution (resolution 678 in the case of the Gulf War).

The significance of power projection, nevertheless, diminishes the further the council moves from a state-on-state agenda. Today, the overwhelming majority of the council's agenda is devoted to intrastate conflict. In such situations, the limits of national power are readily exposed. Moreover, the current permanent membership has been disinclined to provide the council with access to their capabilities for peace operations (aside from budgetary contributions). Thus, the majority of the council's activity relies on, and is sustained by, contributions from non-P-5 states. The permanent membership plays a role in commissioning and managing peace operations, but a marginal role in the day-to-day functioning of these operations. In large part, the superior projection capabilities of the P-5 are lost to the council. Therefore, a permanent member's capacity to project power holds utility for the council only if: (a) it is placed at the disposal of the council; or (b) used to assist in the implementation of a resolution.

Democratization and inclusion

Majority rule is commonly held up as a fundamental democratic precept. Democratic legislatures around the world typically operate according to this principle or under a constitutionally mandated super majority (to usurp the tyranny of the majority). Democratic systems, however, are founded on more than the principle of majority rule. At a fundamental level, the power in a democratic system is located in the hands of the people (commonly known as a government of the people), as they are vested with the authority to directly elect representatives to a legislature. There, the representatives make law on behalf of the people in accordance with a country's constitutional processes.

The question remains: how does democracy translate to international organizations? The EU, for example, has enacted a regional parliament (lower house), which fulfils the legislative function of the union. The parliament is the only such international body that permits direct election of representatives. International organizations are by their very nature intergovernmental—comprised of member-states (independent sovereign states) rather than representatives directly elected by a global electorate. For this simple reason, the translation of the principles of democracy to the international level is a difficult leap to make. The domestic analogy is not entirely suitable, because it is impossible to apply concepts such as the separation of powers, the rule of law, and responsible government.

Several UN fora operate on a set of principles that might be termed nominally democratic. For instance, the General Assembly's one state, one vote procedure means that decisions can be carried on a simple majority or super majority vote (two-thirds). The council, on the other hand, is in fact a highly undemocratic institution when compared to the General Assembly. The veto affords permanent members the power to block council action, even if every other member is in agreement. To many member-states, the council has long been considered exclusionary, opaque, and unaccountable. These behaviors or attributes are often presented as evidence of a democratic deficit. In principle, a democratic deficit occurs "when ostensibly democratic organizations or institutions in fact fall short of fulfilling what are believed to be the principles of democracy."[20] The council is not, and does not purport to be a democratic institution. Whether the membership at large holds the expectation of democratization is difficult to determine. International society is profoundly undemocratic. The inequality embedded in the design of the council privileges five members over all others. The smaller and middle powers consented to the system, and effectively traded the privileges of veto for a workable organization.

In representative democracies, those elected to the legislature nominally speak on behalf of those who have elected them (i.e. their constituents). Elected representatives represent their constituents for a finite period of time. Hence, the concept of the multi-party election resides at the core of every parliamentary democracy. Elections present electors with an active choice about who represents them in parliament. In a similar manner, Security Council elections present members of the General Assembly with an active choice about which countries represent them on the council (presently for two-year terms). In other words, new permanency inhibits active choice, while renewability allows for it.

Participation

The active participation of member-states in the decision-making processes of the council might be considered an exercise in democratization.

The concept of active participation might also imply deliberation (as a form of deliberative democracy). Sabine Hassler has argued that, "better representation would allow different groups to articulate, theorize and politicize their own interests in the Council."[21] In a way, enlargement would grant an increased number of member-states the right to participate in council decision-making, crediting the council in deliberative legitimacy. On this basis, the legitimacy of decisions is not merely prefaced on an aggregation of preferences (i.e. voting), but on the inclusion of key non-council members in deliberations.

In terms of pure participation, an expansion of the council would evidently lead to the participation of members—likely an additional 10. New permanency would widen the circle to include emerging powers from the global south. These new members, holding diverse foreign policy perspectives and strategic cultures, would be actively involved in council deliberations, and their participation, in theory, could serve to legitimize outcomes and improve outputs. The same argument, vis-à-vis participation, can be made on behalf of the renewable seat proposal of the UfC. A renewable seat model would allow for the same level of participation as the G4 model—25 seats. Yet, the exclusivity of new permanency works to limit potential participation. The existence of renewable seats would permit the election, and therefore, the participation of other members (middle powers and regional powers) for extended periods. In numerical terms, the UfC model offers more options for a larger number of members to actively participate on the council; 20 elected seat options for 193 members as opposed to new permanency's 14 seat options for 182 members.

Accountability

In domestic politics, elected representatives are held to account by their electors (the public). This direct accountability is exercised at the ballot box at the end of every term of government (i.e. vote). By voting, the public makes a judgement regarding the performance of elected representatives. The council operates in the rarefied air of international relations, and in many respects, it is a law unto itself; it operates beyond the bounds of international law and is not subject to formal accountability mechanisms. The E-10 can be informally held to account by the membership at large. If elected members perform poorly, future bids may be adversely affected. The permanent five, on the other hand, serve on the council in perpetuity, and although their collective performance is often decried, the membership at large has no avenue for recourse. Likewise, the proposed new cadre of permanent members would not be held to account for their performance. The alternate UfC proposal would provide a greater level of accountability. Plainly, members holding renewable seats (four-year terms or more) would be eminently more accountable than would a P-11.

Would new permanency constitute an exercise in democratization? Firstly, the addition of new permanent members would clearly make the council inclusive of four powerful voices of the global south (India, Brazil, and two African nations). Secondly, affording these new permanent members veto power would disperse power, to a degree. Nevertheless, it would still amount to a concentration of power, albeit in the hands of 11 members rather than the current five. Thirdly, new permanent members would not be held to account to the membership at large. The argument of some permanent representatives within the UfC is that, "if these countries [the G4 + 2] are so significant the rest of the members will keep electing them."[22] The argument for renewable seats is a sound one: if members perform, the membership will continue to elect them; and if they do not perform well, then the membership will deny them a seat at the table. Finally, as discussed in the sections above, new permanency falls down in a number of critical areas vis-à-vis democratization—representation, participation, and accountability.

Would new permanency diminish the role of elected members and thereby inhibit constructive deliberation? The current permanent members do not have a monopoly on constructive input, and neither would an expanded cohort of permanent members. There is a fear, held by some permanent representatives, that a P-11 will largely consult among themselves rather than with the broader membership of the council. The danger of power concentration is that the council deprives itself of the innovation and productive diplomacy of many of the middle and smaller powers. If the locus of power is retained by a P-11, the more difficult it will be for other countries to make constructive contributions.

Efficiency, unanimity and "lowest common denominator-ism"

The council of 15 acts as an executive organ on matters concerning the maintenance of international peace and security. It is conferred with this responsibility and acts on behalf of the membership at large for reasons of promptness and effectiveness. For the drafters at Dumbarton Oaks, a small and manageable body was desirable for reasons of efficiency. Plainly, the larger the decision-making body is, the harder it is for that body to make decisions. As one former permanent representative has argued, "There is a simple numbers reality, as we would sit in council, and 80% of the meetings are closed and rightly so, but when [Country A] would intervene for the seventh time at four o'clock in the morning on [a situation], my patience would be strained. And that's with fifteen. At 24, 25, pick your number…imagine."[23]

A larger council would be a more inefficient, unless the working methods of the Council were to be altered. As Eward C. Luck has suggested a "deficits in working methods would be even more apparent in an expanded Council."[24] As yet, few have asked the question: how would an expanded council efficiently operate day-to-day? In spite of Luck's warning, the UfC, G4, L-69, C-10, and other coalitions advocating for expansion have yet to adequately respond to the dilemma. Although many of the plans promulgated by the G4 and the UfC have referenced working methods reform, the references show a lack of imagination and a lack of concern. It appears that consideration of the working methods of an expanded council is a distraction from the main game. The two G4 working methods propositions largely echo the proposals of more strident working methods reform advocates. Firstly, the proposals suggest a rather reasonable stipulation that would "ensure that non-permanent members of the enlarged Security Council hold the Presidency of the council at least once during their tenure."[25] Secondly, in the interests of transparency and inclusiveness, the G4 suggest that "the enlarged Council would be encouraged to, inter alia, meet, as a general rule, in a public format."[26] Thirdly, the group proposes that the council "make more effective use of informal interactive dialogues; hold open debates on the issue of working methods; hold more regular and timely consultations with troop, police and financial contributing countries of UN peacekeeping missions."[27]

Unanimity and consensus

Some view the council's preference for unanimity as being synonymous with consensus decision-making.[28] This is a popular misconception, however. In fact, consensus decision-making implies not a simple vote, but a commitment to find solutions that the whole can support. Members of the whole can also agree to disagree with the substance of a decision, yet still allow a decision to be adopted. Within NATO, for instance, which practices consensus decision-making, there is no voting. Instead, the NATO Secretary-General facilitates consultations between member-states "until a decision that is acceptable to all is reached."[29] Such a system is cooperative by nature, underlined by shared values, a strategic like-mindedness, and the existence of mutual trust. The council, on the other hand, is quite a different decision-making body, which is governed by procedures of voting stipulated in Article 27 of the charter.

Since the end of the Cold War, the council has placed a premium on unanimity. This is not to say that council resolutions have not been adopted unanimously. Indeed, two of the council's key decisions of the post–Cold War era attracted abstentions—authorizations of the Gulf War (resolution 678) and the Libyan no-fly zone (resolution 1973). Unanimity implies that the adopted decision is an expression of the collective will of the decision-making body. The argument for unanimity is also an argument for solidarity or "a united voice," which in turn, makes it more difficult for a "party targeted by the decision to play Council members against each other."[30] On the other hand, a premium on unanimity can contribute to the emergence of lowest common denominator-ism: a process whereby the clarity, strength, quality, and potential efficacy of a decision is diluted by a desire to achieve its near-universal acceptance. One former permanent representative explains the problem inherent to some council negotiations: "It tends to be a case of regressive negotiations. In any negotiation, it is going to come down on that which people can agree on. Things become vague … which becomes a problem when you're talking about a peacekeeping mandate."[31]

It is difficult to forecast the likely political undercurrents of an expanded council, but under both new permanency and renewability, the council could be subject to a range of potentially negative negotiating dynamics. If unanimity in decision-making were to be adopted in the council of 25 (in accordance with current practice), lowest common denominator-ism would clearly affect the quality of council decisions. Unless council members were to practice a less fervent commitment to their respective positions (and instead defer to the power of the better argument), council decisions may well be compromised; as Lawrence Freeman has suggested, "the accommodation of different interests and perspectives can result in a compromised product."[32]

One senior source described the 2011 council, which featured G4 aspirants India, Brazil, and Germany, as "terrible" with the many members "throwing their weight around for the sake of it."[33]

> More than 20 will massively enhance the power of the P-5; more deals will be done privately. The fix among them will be in. 'This is going to happen or it's not going to happen' and the rest is just show … As more and more irrelevant people jabber on, it will enhance the authority of those who have permanency and veto.[34]

As expressed in the excerpt above, the fear of some elected members is that new permanency will diminish their power to influence outcomes.

This may seem perverse, but as Barry O'Neil suggests, "granting more seats to the nonveto players can diminish their total power [in the Security Council]."[35] A council of 25 would require a likely majority of 15 to carry decisions. If the unanimity principle were to be discarded, fewer elected members would be required to adopt resolutions. Theoretically, the P-5 might only need to court a limited number of elected members to gain a majority.

In an expanded council with new permanent members, the nexus of power would still be retained by the veto-wielding P-5. Under these circumstances, a graduated process of consultations might gain a foothold. Unless the P-5 relinquished their penholder rights, the P-5 would continue to consult among themselves on first drafts in order to negotiate the veto test. The second stage of the process might possibly see the new P-6 (permanent without veto) consulted on heavily scrutinized P-5 drafts. The elected members (E-14) and non-council members would be consulted at the end of the process. The problem with this process of negotiation is its obvious inefficiencies and the continued lack of deliberative appeal.

Contribution to the maintenance of international peace and security

According to the United States, new permanency should only be extended on the basis of candidate country's "willingness to commit to the maintenance of peace and security."[36] The question remains, how can contributions (Article 23) be judged? Several proposed criteria have sought to operationalize the language of Article 23. The *High-Level Panel on Threats, Challenges and Change* offered a number of criteria that could be used to breathe life into Article 23:

> Increase the involvement in decision-making of those who contribute most to the United Nations financially, militarily and diplomatically—specifically in terms of contributions to the United Nations assessed budgets, participation in mandated peace operations, contributions to voluntary activities of the United Nations in the areas of security and development, and diplomatic activities in support of the United Nations objectives and mandates.[37]

On the question of new permanent or longer-term seats, the panel suggested the following criteria:

> Those States that are among the top three financial contributors in their relevant regional area to the regular budget, or the top three

voluntary contributors from their regional area, or the top three troop contributors from their regional area to United Nations peacekeeping missions.[38]

The predominately quantitative criterion offered by the high level panel is an extension of the heavy lifters argument outlined above. Another school of thought offers a more qualitative approach, prefaced on the rather fundamental question: what makes an effective member of the council? The model of agency, presented in chapter two, suggests that effective E-10 members are those that provide leadership, take risks, and expend political capital and resources in a bid to contribute meaningfully to the council's agenda. Such members usually seek out "opportunities to be effective."[39] Effective members of the council have been known to exploit these opportunities through niche diplomacy and innovative interventions. Hence, it can be argued that the system actually relies less on the objective power of states and more on a state's capacity for innovation. The most effective elected members of the council are quite often middle powers (emerging and traditional) that have positioned themselves as norm entrepreneurs, catalysts, facilitators, and mediators. These middle powers are afforded considerable latitude at the UN on some issues, because quite simply, "they're not trying to run the world."[40]

Japan and Germany are the second- and the third-ranked contributors to the UN general budget. India is a major contributor to UN peacekeeping, while Brazil provides the United Nations Stabilisation Mission in Haiti (MINUSTAH) with military backing. While acknowledging their sizable contributions, some have criticized the aspirant's lack of diplomatic imagination at the UN and in the council. One former permanent representative put the criticism rather bluntly:

> Does Germany have good ideas about anything? It's very similar to the Japanese. The Japanese desperately want a permanent seat. But is the Japanese track record at the UN any good? Are they known for innovative, forceful, farsighted, brave interventions? No they're not. Nor are the Germans.[41]

In his assessment of Australia's performance on the council, Richard Gowan made reference to several aspirants (as a point of comparison), stating that, "in recent years major powers including Brazil and India have passed through the council without leaving any substantial legacy."[42] The performance of members is obviously highly subjective. Others would argue quite differently. Germany's last foray into the council was described "worse than even the greatest pessimists had expected,"[43] with much of the attention focused on its infamous abstention on resolution 1973. Unfortunately, for Germany, this single vote seemingly overshadowed its entire term. Yet, to its credit, Germany bravely pursued a presidential statement on climate change and sought to contribute to the modernization of Afghanistan policy, while also tackling the children and armed conflict agenda. India during its 2011–2012 term on the council was "able to leave a footprint on some of the UNSC's work—particularly on counter-terrorism, piracy and peacekeeping."[44] Japan too should be recognized for its efforts toward to the promotion of working methods reforms. Note 507 in 2006 and then subsequently in 2010 were landmark documents, albeit on the fringes of the council's substantive agenda.

In spite of the sometimes-positive performance appraisals, the balance of opinion tends towards the negative. As past performance on the council are seen as the best indicator of future performance, many are decidedly lukewarm about the possibility of new permanency. However, there is a possibility that permanency might positively affect the disposition of the aspirants. A permanent seat would furnish the aspirants with credentials, as well as the expectations of the membership in regards to the exercise of leadership and the expenditure of political will and resources. It could well be argued that permanency might allow aspirant countries to better express their role at the UN, empowering their foreign policies and wedding them more firmly to the UN peace and security agenda. The foreign services of the newly minted permanent members would almost certainly equip their respective missions in New York with ample diplomatic resources.

The personal agency of permanent representatives (and the capacity of their permanent missions) should also not be discounted. Personal agency plays an important role in shaping public perceptions of a country's credibility at the UN. Those permanent missions more practiced or adept in the art of diplomacy in a multilateral setting attract more favorable reviews from their peers. Furthermore, the combination of a strong personal agency and cogent UN policies applies a multiplier effect to a country's efforts in New York. More often than not, those countries possessing a coherent UN policy informed by incisive thinking, generally exercise greater influence of decision-making processes at the UN (through the power of a better argument).

France and the UK, understanding the mood concerning their continued position as permanent members, have in effect relinquished their vetoes and have sought to become "indispensable" members of the council.[45] For the aspirants, breaking into the existing club will not require them to necessarily unseat the French or the British; each must be able to offer something of unique value to the council. The rules of the game will not change to accommodate the aspirants, if they do not succeed in first establishing their credibility with the existing P-5.

Conclusion

This chapter has canvassed the arguments for enlargement of the council under the model proposed by the G4. Although promoted as for its positive potential, new permanency could have the opposite effect. One former permanent representative invoked the Swahili proverb, when explaining the precarious position of the smaller and middle powers in an enlarged council: whether the elephants fight or make love, the grass will still suffer. Would not the smaller and middle powers be marginalized in a larger council? Unless the larger, more powerful states commit to "not throwing their weight around" the collective interest will not be adequately served.[46] Enlargement, it has been argued, may induce paralysis, inhibit democratic accountability, and compromise council outputs. The quality of discussions is not automatically improved by having more seats around the table.

Notes

1 Oxford English Dictionary, Definition of "Reform," (Oxford University Press, 2013).
2 Stephen M. Walt, "The U.N. Security Council. What's Up With That?," *Foreign Policy*, 7 April 2015. http://foreignpolicy.com/2015/04/07/the-u-n-security-council-whats-up-with-that/.
3 The Elders, "Kofi Annan: A Stronger UN," https://www.facebook.com/theElders?rf=119376074812645.
4 Ian Hurd, "Myths of Membership: The Politics of Legitimation in UN Security Council Reform," *Global Governance* 14, No. 2 (April–June 2008): 206.
5 Hurd, "Myths of Membership," 210.
6 Kofi Annan, "We Cannot Be Prosperous at the Expense of the Other, (interview for *RT World's Apart*), 2015. http://theelders.org/article/kofi-annan-we-cannot-be-prosperous-expense-other.
7 Sabine Hassler, *Reforming the UN Security Council membership: The illusion of representativeness* (Abingdon: Routledge, 2013), 162.
8 Ramesh Thakur, "Introduction: UN Electoral Groupings Reform" in *What Is Equitable Geographic Representation in the Twenty-first Century*, ed. Ramesh Thakur (Tokyo: UNU, 1999), 3.
9 Hassler, *Reforming the UN Security Council Membership*, 88.
10 Andrew Linklater and Hidemi Suganami, *The English School of International Relations: A Contemporary Reassessment* (New York: Cambridge University Press, 2006), 216.

11 Hurd, "Myths of Membership," 205.
12 John Lewis Gaddis, *The United States and the Origins of the Cold War*, (New York: Columbia University Press, 1972), 24.
13 Gaddis, *The United States and the Origins of the Cold War*.
14 Brian Urquhart, "Looking for the Sheriff," *New York Review of Books* 45, no. 12 (July 1998).
15 Security Council resolution 1970, 26 February 2011.
16 Security Council resolution 1769, 31 July 2007.
17 Hassler, *Reforming the UN Security Council membership*.
18 Robert Stewart-Ingersoll and Derrick Frazier, *Regional Powers and Security Orders: A Theoretical Framework* (Abingdon: Routledge, 2012), 125.
19 Barry Leonard, ed., *Department of Defense Dictionary of Military and Associated Terms* (Washington, DC: DOD, 2010), 367.
20 Sanford Levinson, "How the United States Constitution Contributes to the Democratic Deficit in America, 55 Drake L." *Rev* 859 (2007): 860.
21 Hassler, *Reforming the UN Security Council Membership*, 94.
22 Anonymous Interviewee, Interview with Author, June 2011.
23 Anonymous Interviewee, Interview with Author, June 2011.
24 Edward C. Luck, *UN Security Council: Practice and Promise* (Abingdon: Routledge, 2006), 122.
25 Intergovernmental Negotiations on the Question of Equitable Representation on and Increase in the Membership of the Security Council and Related Matters, *Framework Document,* 2015. http://www.un.org/en/ga/president/69/letters/130515_ign-sc.pdf.
26 Intergovernmental Negotiations on the Question of Equitable Representation on and Increase in the Membership of the Security Council and Related Matters, *Framework Document.*
27 Intergovernmental Negotiations on the Question of Equitable Representation on and Increase in the Membership of the Security Council and Related Matters, *Framework Document.*
28 Security Council Report has suggested that the Council practices consensus decision-making. However, this is not the case. Consensus decision-making does not rely on voting.
29 North Atlantic Treaty Organization, *Consensus Decision-Making at NATO,* 2014 http://www.nato.int/cps/en/natolive/topics_49178.htm.
30 Security Council Report, *In Hindsight: Consensus in the Security Council,* 2014 http://www.securitycouncilreport.org/monthly-forecast/2014-01/in_hindsight_consensus_in_the_security_council.php?print=true.
31 Anonymous Interviewee, Interview with Author, June 2011.
32 Lawrence Freedman, *Strategy: A History* (New York: Oxford University Press, 2013), 612.
33 Anonymous Interviewee, Interview with Author, June 2011.
34 Anonymous Interviewee, Interview with Author, June 2011.
35 Barry O'Neill, "Power and Satisfaction in the United Nations Security Council," *The Journal of Conflict Resolution* 40, no. 2 (1996): 236.
36 UN General Assembly, *Speakers, Voicing Frustration at Lack of Progress, Call for Security Council Reforms to Reflect Current Political Realities,* 2014. http://www.un.org/press/en/2014/ga11583.doc.htm.
37 High-Level Panel on Threats Challenges and Change, *A More Secure World: Our Shared Responsibility* (New York: United Nations, 2004), 80.

38 High-Level Panel on Threats Challenges and Change, *A More Secure World,* 82.
39 Anonymous Interviewee, Interview with Author, June 2011.
40 Anonymous Interviewee, Interview with Author, June 2011.
41 Anonymous Interviewee, Interview with Author, June 2011.
42 Richard Gowan, *Australia in the UN Security Council* (Sydney: The Lowy Institute for International Policy, 2013), 4.
43 Richard Gowan, *Germany and the Security Council: Neither too strong nor too weak*, 2013. http://www.dgvn.de/fileadmin/user_upload/PUBLIKA TIONEN/Zeitschrift_VN/VN_2013/Gowan_Germany_and_UNSC_Eng._ FINAL.pdf.
44 Rohan Mukherjee and David Malone, "India and the UN Security Council: An Ambiguous Tale," *Economic and Political Weekly* (20 July 2013): 115.
45 Anonymous Interviewee, Interview with Author, June 2011.
46 Anonymous Interviewee, Interview with Author, June 2011.

5   Working methods reform

adhoc - when necessary or needed!

- **Note 507**
- **Small Five (S-5) and the Accountability, Coherence, and Transparency Group (ACT)**
- **Working methods: logic, utility, implementation, and acceptance**
- **Public meetings**
- **Informal fora**
- **The role of the president, thematic debates and penholders**
- **Subsidiary bodies**
- **The veto**
- **Conclusion**

The council's working methods are based on the Provisional Rules of Procedure (1982) and a range of ad-hoc and evolved practices. Article 30 of the charter makes clear that the council is the "master of its own procedure,"[1] as it states, "the Security Council shall adopt its own rules of procedure."[2] The work of deciding on the rules of procedure was left to the Executive Committee of the Preparatory Commission, and then later the Security Council itself. On 24 June 1946, the council finally agreed on a set of 60 provisional rules of procedure. Albeit for a few minor revisions, the rules have remained virtually unchanged. The last revision was conducted in 1982 when Arabic was included as an official language of the UN. The rules have never been formally adopted. Advocates of the provisional rules suggest that "they give the Council more flexibility and allow it to adapt better and faster to the changing international environment."[3] Others believe the rules give the P-5 a tactical advantage, a metaphorical rug to be pulled out from under any difficult elected member.

On the whole, working methods reform is seen as the unsexy cousin of the mainstream reform debate. Yet a growing number of member-states have come to realize the great potential for working methods reform. Firstly, new initiatives or changes to working methods do not require charter amendment. Secondly, working methods reforms, in many cases, seek to address the real defects that currently inhibit the council's agency. Reform of working methods, if done well, would have more of an "immediate effect" than expansion.[4] Hence, this area of potential reform represents arguably most fertile ground for meaningful improvement. Through the work the Informal Working Group on Documentation and Other Procedural Questions (IWG) and other subsidiary bodies of the council, a number of reforms have been introduced. Implementation has been patchy, however. Generally, the council has innovated through the initiative of its elected members. However, these innovative practices have at times been misused, overused, or disused.

This chapter will be divided into two broad sections. The first section provides an examination of the Note 507, the role of the IWG, and the initiatives of the S-5/ACT. The second section analyzes the various working methods reforms implemented, slated, or proposed, such as meeting formats; the role of the penholder and presidency; and subsidiary bodies. A number of questions will be posed of each: what is the logic of the working method? Does the method have utility? Has the working method taken hold? Is there resistance to its introduction or its continuation?

Note 507

The working methods of the council are jealously guarded by its members under Article 30. The history of the debate suggests that reform of the council's practices originate from within the council. Since 2006, a host of elected members have taken up the campaign for improved working methods. Their stalwart has been Japan. Working within an enhanced IGW (a 12-month chair), Japan codified the framework for discussions on improvements. Perhaps, the most important development in the "slow and ... tortured process"[5] of working methods reform was the adoption of Note 507 under the IWG presidency of Japan in 2006. In broad terms, the note sought to "enhance the efficiency and transparency of the council's work, as well as the interaction and dialogue with non-council members."[6] In specific terms, it provided a suite of 63 working methods proposals, many "previously agreed by the Council."[7] Others were original suggestions. In 2010, Note 507 was updated. A summary of the proposals is organized thematically below.

- **Transparency:** The note concluded that the council must become more open to the membership at large. Participation promotes transparency and accountability. Note 507 urged the council to "publicize its decisions and other relevant information" through the use of "correspondence, websites, outreach activities."[8] The founding of Security Council Report in 2004 went some way toward promoting freedom of information regarding council meetings and activities. The council's own website also features monthly progams of work, the council repertoire, meeting records, and other documents.

- **Stakeholders:** The note touched on arguably the key foci of the working methods reform agenda—engagement with non-council members (TCCs/PCCs, "specifically affected, neighbouring States and countries with particular contributions to make, as well as with regional organizations and Groups of Friends").[9] The participation of key stakeholders in meetings and informal consultations fosters "closer cooperation between the Council and those actors."[10] It makes perfect sense for the council to involve key stakeholders for one simple reason: they are the most intimately involved in the implementation of council decisions. Improving two-way access (input and information) to briefings, meetings, informal consultations, and progams of work are assessed in the note as being of critically importance.

- **Briefings and reports:** Note 507 sets a standard six-month reporting period and directs the Secretariat to provide the council concise reports to be circulated in advance of consideration. The council is said to encourage recommendations regarding mandate and long-term strategy. The note also encourages the production of tentative forecasts, the holding of ad-hoc briefings by the Secretariat, and informal briefings by chairs of subsidiary bodies.

- **Speakers and interactivity:** To put a stop to repetitious and long-winded speeches, Note 507 suggests a cessation of the reiteration of similar statements, as well as the imposition of a five-minute time limit on statements. Furthermore, the note suggested that adherence to the speaker's list should not come at the expense of interactivity—a premium must be placed on interactivity.

- **Meetings:** The note reissues a long-standing mantra "increase resource to open meetings."[11] The use of open meetings in the early consideration of a matter is highlighted. The note suggests a rather common-sense protocol—non-members with a direct interest in an outcome should speak before council members.

- The council's adoption of working methods reforms envisaged in Note 507 has been inconsistent. The council, nevertheless, has continued to innovate, as it always has. In recent years, the council has introduced a range of new meeting formats in an effort to improve processes and outcomes. A range of new formats has also emerged, including wrap-up sessions, informal interactive discussion/dialogue, the Kosovo model, and the informal dialogue.

Small Five (S-5) and the Accountability, Coherence, and Transparency Group (ACT)

The S-5 tried working methods reforms from outside of the council. The group drafted a resolution (A/60/L.49) of 17 March 2006 containing 19 measures. The draft resolution, however, never generated any traction, and was not even acknowledged by the P-5 or the council. The S-5 focused in on five key issues (1) the relationship with the General Assembly; (2) the effectiveness of decisions; (3) the relationship with subsidiary bodies; (4) the operations mandated by the council: governance and accountability; (5) and the appointment of the UN Secretary-General. In May 2012, the S-5 proposed a suite of 20 working methods reforms (A/66/L.42/Rev.2). The most controversial aspect of the resolution was the insistence that the P-5 explain their vetoes to the membership and refrain from exercising their veto power to prevent council action on mass atrocity crimes and genocide. The S-5 had kicked a metaphorical hornet's nest. The P-5 rebuked the S-5, and explained that the working methods of the council were strictly the domain of the council, and that any change to its working methods would require a two-thirds majority in the General Assembly. The S-5 beat a hasty retreat, reforming a year later as the Accountability Coherence and Transparency Group (ACT).

With a broader membership,[12] the new working methods coalition adopted a "modest, pragmatic, and non-confrontational approach"[13] to their work. Like its predecessor, the ACT coalition concerns itself solely with working methods reforms and calls for a "more transparent, efficient, inclusive, coherent, legitimate and accountable."[14] In doing so, the group has removed itself from the debates on new permanency and expansion.

Working methods: logic, utility, implementation, and acceptance

Working methods are primarily focused on deliberation. The following section will profile each of the key working methods of the council by posing a set of questions:

- What is the internal logic of the method? How does it work? What is its aim?

- What is the utility of the method?
- Have there been changes in the way the method has been used by the council over the course of time?
- Has the method gained acceptance by the council? What are the sources of resistance?

Public meetings

Rule 48 of the Provisional Rules of Procedure states that, "unless it decides otherwise, the Security Council shall meet in public."[15] Throughout the Cold War, the council would usually met once a week. The theater of the Cold War was played out in the full view of the public. During the Cuban Missile Crisis, there was standing room only in the council chamber as delegates clambered to view aerial photographs of purported Soviet missile sites presented by the US delegation.[16] Member-states often hold up public meetings as the bastion of transparency. However, most public meetings nowadays are downright dry or boring. They are poorly attended and not particularly revealing. This is because all of the critical decisions are made behind closed doors, and even beyond the UN itself in conference rooms across midtown Manhattan. There are four public meetings formats: briefing, debate, open debate, and adoption.

Briefings

A briefing involves only members of council and the briefer/briefers. In line with this restriction, only council members can deliver statements following briefings. In short, the aim of a briefing is to inform the council of a particular situation or convey information. The 7468th meeting of the council on 23 June 2015 is a contemporary example of a briefing. The meeting convened to hear a briefing from Abdoulaye Diop (Malian Minister for Foreign Affairs) and Mongi Hamdi (SRSG for Mali and Head of MINUSMA) concerning the situation in Mali. As indicated in the example, affected states and Secretariat officials (SRSGs, USGs) can be invited by the council to participate in a briefing. Others can also be invited to brief the council, including the chairs of the Peacebuilding Commission's (PBC) country-specific configurations.

In the 1990s, Secretariat officials provided a daily high-level comprehensive situational briefing to the council. The council abandoned the practice in the early 2000s. The United States attempted to resurrect the practice in February 2006 by scheduling a daily briefing at the front end of AM consultations. The revived briefings were short-lived.

Debates and open debates

A debate is a public meeting that involves the participation of the full council and invited non-council members: those members "that are directly concerned or affected or have special interest in the matter under consideration may be invited to participate in the discussion upon their request."[17] In practice, debates allow for the participation of states intimately involved in the situation or that have a stake in the intervention. This might include the members of the group of friends, neighboring states, key donors, and mediator states.

The open debate is the most inclusive of all meeting formats. Under the open-debate format, any non-council member can request an invitation to speak. The format is usually invoked when the council is adopting a resolution on a thematic topic, such as women, peace, and security (resolution 1325) or security sector reform (SSR) (resolution 2151). The open debate on SSR featured a speaker list of 40 representatives including the head of the EU delegation (allowed under Rule 39 of the provisional rules of procedure). Many thematic and some country- or region-specific open debates extend for many hours and sometimes up to two sessions—morning and afternoon.

Use of the term debate seems to imply an exchange of views or a robust consideration of a possible course of action. Unfortunately, Security Council debates and open debates are debates in name only. A typical open-debate, for instance, hears a series of short pre-prepared statements read verbatim by representatives, one after another. There are no impromptu exchanges of view or moments of interactivity. During its presidency in November 2000, the Netherlands distributed a concept note entitled, "No Exit without Strategy,"[18] intended for use as a guide for an open-debate on peace operations. The distribution of such a frank and fearless note was a particularly welcome innovation.

Informal fora

Council members recognize the interactive deficit, and as a result, many of the recent innovative practices have been labeled as interactive fora. The most commonly utilized format is informal consultations of the whole. The eight months from January to August 2015 saw, on average, 13 consultations, nine briefings, seven public meetings (adoptions, open debates, and debates) held per month. The council's reliance on informal consultations is criticized by some and lauded by others. The critics view informal consultations as the greatest impediment to transparency; some have gone as far as to argue that the practice contributes to the widening of the gap between council members and the membership at large. The lack of written record-taking "does not contribute to the enhancement of the credibility of the Council,"[19] nor is the practice conducive to setting accountability or the promotion of consistency in decision-making.

At the UN, there exists a tension between transparency and secrecy. Throughout the work of the preparatory commission, many delegates, fearful of substantial decisions made behind closed doors, railed against the concept of private consultations. One unnamed delegate aptly summarized the fear, "the whole purpose of the United Nations was to minimize secret diplomacy, and that states making honest and sincere decisions had no reason to be afraid of publicity."[20] One of the constants of multilateral diplomacy is the need for compromise. The system is paralyzed without it. If the council's public meetings were to become a staple, members of the council holding to divergent views might be less inclined to abandon their positions or moderate for fear of losing their prestige or honor. Private meetings, aside from their problems, offer members an opportunity to save face when altering their positions. One former permanent representative summarizes the dilemma:

> It is much harder to reach compromises in public than in private ... accountability, yes, transparency, yes, with some recognition that quite a bit of work has to be done before you get to the point of dealing with it in public, because otherwise you lock in positions rather than allow for accommodations. Because you always need to remember that you could be wrong, maybe your position doesn't make sense.[21]

The growing problem with informal consultations has been their apparent lack of interactivity. It has been noted that much like public meetings, informal consultations have been infected by the tendencies of members toward ritualistic, rhetorical statements over conversations of substance. Reports indicate that, "several Presidents of the council have tried to introduce, largely unsuccessfully, more interactivity and spontaneity into Council consultations."[22] The malady has infected other meeting formats too, as will be discussed below. The interactivity deficit is arguably the most threatening disorder of the council.

Wrap-up session

The concept of wrap-up session was proposed by Bangladeshi in March 2000. The mission invited Kofi Annan into informal consultations to provide a statement of "his own views on the priorities and the course of action on some of the issues before the Council."[23] The Secretary-General's briefing was later accompanied by a reflective synopsis of the Bangladeshi presidency presented as an annex to a letter from the permanent mission of Bangladesh (S/2000/670).[24] Over the course of the early 2000s, presidents of the council appropriated the concept and made alterations to the format to suit their purposes or the content of discussions. Some wrap-up sessions were held in public (attended by non-council members and featuring briefings of senior UN officials), while others were private (although still made open to non-council members). Generally, prior to each meeting, either an informal concept note, non-paper, or advance guidelines were circulated to members. Occasionally, following certain meetings, a short note was provided which summarized the matters discussed.

By 2004, the mood had turned against the sessions; it was said that some members were "not hostile, but also not enthusiastic,"[25] although the UK permanent representative spoke of the sessions as being "quite useful."[26] A sharp decline in the number of sessions was noted through 2004 and 2005, and by 2009, the wrap-up session agenda item was deleted from the seizure list. However, in February 2011, Brazil chose to revive the practice. Enthusiasm for the practice flourished among non-council members, with many calling the sessions an exercise in accountability. The Finnish permanent representative aptly summed up the new mood, stating that "interactive wrap-up sessions at the end of each month would enhance information-sharing and open-ness."[27] In early 2015, Malaysia, France, and Chile all chose to convene public sessions. Since the revival of the wrap-ups, some members, including many of the P-5, have questioned the usefulness of the sessions, particularly those held in public, as council members are seen to be more inclined to voice their criticisms in private. The aim of the sessions is to assess the effectiveness of the council's work and evaluate the implementation of its decisions.

Orientation debates

France first mooted the idea of an orientation debate in the December 1994. In short, the concept aimed to allow member-states to make known their position on a country-specific file prior to the council commencing substantive action. A French aide-mémoire defined the orientation debates in the following terms:

> On taking up a new question or beginning its consideration of an important matter, would give the floor to States' Members of the Organization at their request so as to hear their views on the subject and discuss with them possible courses of action in that regard ... any Member State would have the opportunity to express its views on a problem, directly and publicly, to the Council before the latter defined its position.[28]

A subsequent presidential statement codified the practice stating that:

> as part of its [the Council] efforts to improve the flow of information and the exchange of ideas between members of the Council and other United Nations Member States, that there should be an increased recourse to open meetings, in particular at an early stage in its consideration of a subject.[29]

In line with the presidential statement, both permanent and elected members alike invoked the working method on "a case by case basis."[30] In 1996, orientation debates were utilized to assist the council in the framing of its response to Liberia, Angola, Somalia, and Afghanistan. Despite being lauded as an effective tool, the practice was soon abandoned.

Troop Contributing Countries (TCCs)/Police Contributing Countries (PCCs) meetings

Around 1992, the council began to insert peacekeepers amidst ongoing conflicts in the Balkans and Somalia. Peacekeepers were now routinely called upon to move beyond the traditional scope of blue-helmeted operations. This change in posture exposed troops to greater risks, and in 1993, 251 peacekeepers were killed in the line of duty. Recalling Article 44 of the charter, TCCs began to lobby for greater consultation.[31] The council simply could not ignore the call. In 1994, both "Argentina and New Zealand [elected members of the Council at the time] launched a joint initiative to formalise and enhance the interaction between the TCCs and the Council."[32] Informal private meetings of the council were first convened for the United Nations Protection Force (UNPROFOR) in 1994.

In late 2000, the release of the landmark Brahimi Report pre-cipitated a major rethink on peacekeeping and called for the institu-tionalization of TCC consultations. The council responded to the report by passing an initial resolution (res. 1327) and then a targeted resolution (res. 1353) on the question of strengthening cooperation with troop-contributing countries.[33] A subsequent tranche of council actions built on resolution 1353 laid the foundations for an era of enhanced interaction between TCCs and the council.[34]

First, the Brahimi Report suggested a new way of laying down mandates through early engagement with troop contributors. The report recommended the council "leave in draft form resolutions authorizing missions with sizeable troop levels until such time as the Secretary-General has firm commitments of troops."[35] The recommen-dation was not heeded by the council, which continues to authorize troop ceilings without receiving commitments from troop contributors. Brahimi also recommended that when mandates are formatted or changed, TCCs should be briefed by the Secretariat "on matters affecting the safety and security of their personnel."[36]

Second, the annex to resolution 1353 set out, among other things, three formats for TCC consultations. The resolution created a new formal troop-contributors meeting format (private or public) to con-sider "issues of critical importance to [each] specific peacekeeping operation."[37] The meeting could be convened at a contributor's request, when the new operation was being considered, when the council was considering a renewal/modification/completion of a man-date, or when in a crisis. Third, S/PRST/2001/3 established the Security Council Working Group on Peacekeeping Operations and charged it with the responsibility of improving the triad of cooperation between the Secretariat (principally DPKO), the council and the TCCs.

At the first meeting under the new formalized resolution 1353, a TCC meeting was held to discuss the UN Mission in Ethiopia and Eritrea (UNMEE). Thereafter, meetings were convened on various peacekeeping operations in a committee room and co-chaired by a UN secretariat official and the council president. Best practice would see TCCs notified of meetings "in good time,"[38] background notes circu-lated in advance of the meeting, and most importantly, TCCs would be notified well in advance of modifications or renewal of mandates.

Like many of the council fora, the TCC meetings have not been immune to a lack of interactivity, with many TCCs complaining that the consultations "had become pro forma and ritualistic, instead of a real exchange of perspectives."[39] Furthermore, although the meetings afforded a useful opportunity to engage the council, some troop contributors have felt the council was ignoring their views. On the other side, some council members have objected to the passivity of certain TCCs, the complete absence of certain TCC delegations, and the poorly briefed presence of other representatives.

Arria-formula meeting

In March 1992, Diego Arria of Venezuela invited a Croatian priest, Fra Joko Zovko, to testify to the council over coffee in the delegates' lounge. From this rather innocuous beginning, the Arria Formula sessions were born. The Arria Formula sessions are intended as

> very informal, confidential gatherings which enable Security Council members to have a frank and private exchange of views, within a flexible procedural framework, with persons whom the inviting member or members of the Council (who also act as the facilitators or conveners) believe it would be beneficial to hear and/ or to whom they may wish to convey a message.[40]

In the beginning the format was used as a way of allowing visiting high-level representatives to speak with council members. The likes of Richard Goldstone (Chair of the Goldstone Commission on apartheid in South Africa), Alfredo Cristiani (president of El Salvador), Cyrus Vance (UN Special Envoy to Bosnia), and David Owen (EU representative) were all invited to Arria Formula meetings to informally discuss their respective topics of concern. Later, around 2001, the format changed. High-level representatives were accommodated via other formats (inform interactive dialogues and discussions), and the Arria meetings were opened to non-governmental organizations (Human Rights Watch, Global Witness, and Amnesty International), think tanks (International Crisis Group and NYU's Center on International Cooperation), and even UN goodwill ambassadors (Mia Farrow).

Informal dialogue

In mid-2008, the prosecutor of the ICC alleged that President of the Republic of Sudan Omar al-Bashir bore criminal responsibility for genocide and other mass atrocity crimes relating to the case of Darfur; the Security Council had referred the matter to the ICC in 2005 (resolution 1593). Both the AU and the League of Arab States organizations roundly condemned the Prosecution application. In February

2009, a delegation from both organizations visited New York, seeking to meet with the council.[41] Under Article 16 of the Rome Statute, the council has the power to defer a prosecution for 12 months (renewable). The council yielded to a request and arranged an informal meeting to engage the delegation.

The informal dialogue "allows [the council] to better exchange views with members of the United Nations on situations that concern them directly."[42] Typically the format provides the flexibility for the council to meet with one or more non-council members, as well as delegates from regional organizations, envoys, chairpersons of the Peacebuilding Commission (PBC), and SRSGs. The informal interactive dialogue has, in effect, come to replace the pre-2001 Arria Formula meetings.[43]

Horizon-scanning briefing

The horizon-scanning briefing, a UK initiative, was a relatively new innovation of the council before it was mothballed. As originally conceived, the briefings were designed to accommodate preventive thinking and bring areas of potential conflagration to the council's attention. The council's weaknesses in early warning and prevention have been continually highlighted, but to limited affect. Even the first article of the UN charter is an ode to prevention, stating that the purposes of the UN in the field of peace and security are "to take effective collective measures for the prevention and removal of threats to the peace" and to "bring about by peaceful means...adjustment or settlement of international disputes or situations which might lead to a breach of the peace."[44] The council, however, avoiding the natural sensitivities of states, embraced reaction and rejected anticipatory action and a philosophy of prevention. For these reasons, the horizon-scanning exercise was a unique experiment.

A typical briefing would see the Under-Secretary-General for Political Affairs B. Lynn Pascoe and his successor, Jeffrey Feltman, cover a range of country situations, many of which were not on the council's agenda: Egypt, Gabon, Cameroon, Sri Lanka, Nepal, Libya, Madagascar, the Maldives, Mexico, and Senegal. However, over time the process degenerated. At first, the sessions were highly interactive, relatively speaking. By 2012, they had become a clone of most council meetings—formalized, inflexible, a platform for members to read pre-prepared statements. Furthermore, some members began to feel uneasy about the free-range approach. The Department of Political Affairs (DPA) was in the driver's seat and, so, could potentially raise any issue within the bounds of prudence. This was viewed by the agenda-controlling set as intolerable. The sharp edge of the analysis provided by DPA had been blunted, as had the department's ambition and advocacy around the briefings. An exercise which started out as a rather logical step forward on the question of prevention, ended in political discord and recriminations regarding the format's usefulness.

The role of the president, thematic debates and penholders

Since the early 2000s, elected members have sought to champion thematic causes during their presidencies.[45] For the most part, the permanent members "turn their noses down"[46] at thematic questions. Nevertheless, the elected set continues to use the thematic cause to good effect. The practice of championing thematic resolutions is one way the presidents of the council have sought to exercise meaningful influence over the council agenda. The process typically unfolds as follows. First, the president schedules an open debate on the chosen thematic topic. The debates are usually scheduled for late in the month to lend sufficient time to the negotiation of a resolution or presidential statement. Second, a high level representative of country's government (holding the presidency) visits New York to chair the open debate and wield the gavel (although the minister in question usually departs before the conclusion of the debate). Third, following a set of opening remarks the carefully negotiated resolution or PRST is adopted. As a result, the statements offered after the adoption do not inform the outcome document.

The aim of this practice is twofold. Firstly, the president is seen to be championing a cause on the world stage. Outward appearances are an important consideration for most elected members. Some have even come to view the practice as a cynical ploy designed to garner a "considerable amount of both domestic and international media exposure."[47] Secondly, a thematic open debate and adoption advances the cause of holistic approaches to peace and security.

Penholders

Under the old system of drafting, the British were famous for their ability to produce draft resolutions: "he with the pen wins ... they always have the draft."[48] In 2008, a new system of penholdership emerged to replace the initiative based system. As the term implies, the penholder drafts all resolutions on the topic or situation of concern. In practice, the penholder becomes the de facto leader on the topic. The permanent members decide penholder and chairperson appointments. Customarily, the E-10 preside over sanctions committees, while the permanent members, as the penholders, handle the various country-specific files. France, the United Kingdom, and the United States have, in effect, monopolized the penholder system. As of the start of 2015:

- France held the pen on issues concerning its former colonies CAR, Cote d'Ivoire, Mali, the DRC, Burundi, and the Great Lakes.
- The UK held the pen on Yemen, Cyprus, Sierra Leone, Darfur, Libya, Somalia, peace operations, PoC, and resolution 1325.
- The United States held the pen on counterterrorism (resolutions 1373, 1566 1267 and 1989), Western Sahara, South Sudan, conflict between Sudan and South Sudan, Somali piracy, the Palestinian question, the UN Disengagement Observer Force (UNDOF), Libya, Iraq, Iran, Liberia, Haiti, and DPRK.

In 2015, only a couple of elected members held the pen on country-specific situations: Nigeria on Guinea-Bissau and Spain on Afghanistan. The pens, however, were more widely shared among the E-10 on thematic issues and regional matters: Nigeria on West Africa and Guinea-Bissau; Angola on working methods and peace and security in Africa; Spain on Afghanistan and WMD (weapons of mass destruction) non-proliferation; Malaysia on children and armed conflict; and Chile on the International Court of Justice. Interestingly, on both Kosovo and Bosnia, a rotating Contact and Drafting Group continued to act as the de facto penholder.

Figuratively the approach resembles three concentric circles. Typically the penholder will draft a resolution and then circulate it among the cabal of three (i.e. the first circle). The draft is then circulated to the Russians and Chinese for further negotiation (i.e. the second circle). Once Russia and China reach agreement on the substance of the text, it is finally circulated to the E-10 (i.e. the third circle) with a de facto disclaimer: do not call for amendments that might upset the consensus achieved among the permanent members. A former E-10 permanent representative explains the last part of the process for their perspective:

> They [the permanent members] are not inherently smarter than you [an elected member], but they have been talking about it [the situation], enough to understand the basics. Then they bring it forward into the Council, into the back room, and you do a lot of talking and you try and insert some stuff and you find out whether they can live with it or not … but there may well be things that they might not have thought of. There are only five of them,

they're backed up by pretty big establishments, but there are others [the E-10] who could be expected to add something constructive.[49]

Originally, the penholder system was designed to ensure an efficient division of labor, but the search for so-called efficiency dividends has produced a series of knock-on effects. Firstly, the penholder system has contributed to "a deepening negotiation and consultation gap between the permanent and elected members." In fact, it can be argued that the system is adding to the deliberative deficit, which continues to undermine the legitimacy of the council. Secondly, the practical authority of sanctions committee chairpersonship is undermined by penholder monopolization. The P-3 penholder, as the often self-appointed lead, occupies a position of power, while the E-10 chair occupies a deferential position. Thirdly, the monopolization (or a hoarding of pens) has led, in some instances, to lethargic responses. Sometimes a penholder, burdened with up to a dozen country-specific files, might be concerned with another case or simply might lack the energy to pursue innovative or concert action on a topic of concern. In these instances, "the Council may be delayed or paralysed from taking action."[50]

The penholder system is, nevertheless, born of the practical realities of the council. The permanent members serve continuously, so for continuity's sake, would it not seem fit to extend penholderships to the permanent five? Furthermore, the cabal allows the permanent members to expeditiously iron out their differences on drafts, working around the ever-present veto. A draft initiated from among the E-10 would still need to contend with the same facts. Penholder reform has been mooted. In 2012, Portugal, as chair of the IWG, "circulated a draft note by the President outlining a system under which all Council members would have an opportunity to be penholders or co-penholders."[51] The note encountered resistance and was dropped. The drafting processes of the council are beholden to the P-3, so why would they willingly hand over their power to others? Clearly, relinquishing power is a difficult proposition for all who possess it.

Subsidiary bodies

Under Article 29 of the charter, the council is granted the power to establish subsidiary bodies "as it deems necessary for the performance of its functions."[52] The council has a vast constellation of subsidiary organs: two counterterrorism organs; sixteen sanctions committees (as well as an ombudsman and focal point for delisting); nine ad hoc bodies and standing committees; two international criminal tribunals;

the military staff committee; and the peacebuilding commission. Most of the UN's peace operations (SPMs and PKOs) are also officially subsidiary organs of the council.

Military staff committee (MSC)

As noted in Chapter 1, the UN was supposed to be equipped with a capable military enforcement tool. By signing the charter, member-states had committed to making "available to the Security Council, on its call and in accordance with a special agreement or agreements, armed forces, assistance, and facilities."[53] These forces would be placed under the control of the MSC; a subsidiary body charged with the responsibility "for the strategic direction of any armed forces placed at the disposal of the Security Council."[54] Resolution 1 of the Security Council called for the chiefs of staff of the militaries of the permanent members to meet in London to decide on the procedures of the new MSC. Within two years, the MSC had become untenable. The committee still continues to meet every two weeks, however. Today, the committee has the scope to review mandates (and has done so on a number of occasions), advising on troop strengths, and force generation issues. Sievers and Daws have noted that E-10 members have been invited to attend informal "portions of regularly scheduled meetings,"[55] while representatives from DPA, DPKO, and DFS have also been granted the opportunity to attend.

Formal reform of the committee has been mooted, but never seriously considered. Calls for its abolition have been rejected by the P-5. Interestingly, Russia has led efforts to revive the committee. These efforts, however, have not resulted in any meaningful discussion. Few member-states are actually interested in the MSC, and formal substantive alterations would require charter amendment. Any revival of a functioning military advisory board would need to service the council's constant demands on the peacekeeping front. The MSC is seemingly ill equipped (in terms of membership) and too inflexible (due to charter edicts) to inhabit such a role. An ad hoc board comprising key TCCs and financial contributors might be a more credible peacekeeping advisory fora and TCC conduit.

The veto

Since the end of the Cold War (January 1990 to August 2015), all permanent members have exercised veto restraint. In this 25-year period, 31 vetoes have been exercised by three of the five permanent members (see Appendix 1). France and the UK have not used their vetoes since Panama in December 1989, and it is unlikely that either country would exercise the power of the veto again; at least not without the support of either the US, Russia, or China. The other permanent members have used the veto sparingly, in a relative sense. Since 1990, Russia has used the veto on 13 occasions. Acting alone, Russia has exercised the veto seven times: on Bosnia (twice), Ukraine (twice), Cyrus (twice), and Georgia. Russia and China have employed their vetoes (six times) in tandem: on Syria (four times), and once each on Myanmar and Zimbabwe. Since the mid-2000s, Russia has exercised the veto more regularly than any other permanent member (a total of ten times). The US has used the veto a total of 16 times. The majority—a total of 14—of these vetoes concern matters relating to the situation in the Middle East, including the Palestinian question. The outlier vetoes—a total of two—concerned the situation in Nicaragua and Bosnia. China, on the other hand, has only exercised the veto a total of eight times, in the same period. Only twice has China exercised its veto alone. These vetoes effectively cancelled the mandates of both United Nations Preventive Deployment Force (UNPREDP) in Macedonia and United Nations Verification Mission in Guatemala (MINUGUA) in Central America.

Since 2011, the cases of Libya and Syria have stirred animosities in the council. Four vetoes exercised by Russia, with China in support, are viewed negatively by many member-states. The council's perceived failings on Syria has led a number of member-states to entertain the notion of a moratorium on the veto as it relates to matters concerning mass atrocity crimes. The proposal is not fresh initiative, however. The Canadian government's International Commission on Intervention and State Sovereignty (ICISS) first proposed veto restraint on situations of mass atrocity crimes back in 2001. Suggesting that:

> The Permanent Five members of the Security Council should agree not to apply their veto power, in matters where their vital state interests are not involved, to obstruct the passage of resolutions authorizing military intervention for human protection purposes for which there is otherwise majority support.[56]

Initially, member-states did not respond favorably to the proposal, and so in General Assembly resolution A/RES/60/1 of October 2005 (World Summit Outcome) mention of it was avoided. In 2010, the idea was revived. France has championed the issue in recent times, and has laid out a broad-brush stroke proposal in a New York Times op-ed penned by French Foreign Minister Laurent Fabius. The moratorium proposal can best be described as RtoP veto code of conduct or a "responsibility not to veto," (RNtoV) aimed at preserving "the fundamental credibility of the Security Council, which should be a pillar of peace and stability."[57]

Much like the working methods reforms outlined above, the code of conduct would be relatively simple to implement, because the charter would not need to be altered. Instead, the permanent members would commit to voluntarily regulating their right to veto in situations where mass atrocity crimes have been committed. The commitment would be no more than a non-binding "gentlemen's agreement."[58] If any member were to exercise their veto, the tide of moral indignation would be swift and overwhelming. However, "to be realistically applicable, this code would exclude cases where the vital national interests of a permanent member of the council were at stake."[59] The problem with this condition is obvious: how is national interest defined? If the permanent members were to submit to the code of conduct, this provision would need to be negotiated on a case-by-case basis—a rather intricate process, to be sure.

Who would make the determination? According to the French proposal at least 50 member-states (or around 25 percent of the General Assembly) would call on the UN Secretary-General to make a determination: has a mass crime been committed, in this instance? If the Secretary-General determines that a mass atrocity crime has been committed, then the RtoP veto code of conduct immediately applies. The procedural mechanics remain rather vague and ill defined. Many questions abound. How would a RNtoV scenario play out procedurally? Would the code of conduct cover all resolutions on an agenda item (i.e. every single resolution adopted in relation to a particular situation) or only those resolutions with an RtoP focus (i.e. authorizing military action to halt mass crimes)? Most importantly, would the US, China and Russia submit to a code of conduct?

The US is entertaining the notion, and it is believed that there has been "internal debate within the Obama administration about the merits of the proposal."[60] China and Russia appear ardently opposed to any limitations to the veto; and neither will voluntarily commit to the code of conduct, at this time. In spite of this, International Humanitarian Law (IHL), the Convention on the Prevention and Punishment of the Crime of Genocide (CPPCG), the norm of the RtoP, and the general normative direction of the council clearly continue to exert an influence on the calculations of permanent members, altering the voting patterns. The humanitarian access resolutions concerning the situation in Syria pushed both Russia and China into a potential veto, yet both opted out of exercising their rights. The severe reputational and credibly costs incurred by vetoing humanitarian resolutions were adjudged to be too great to bear for both Russia and China.

Conclusion

From the working methods profiled above, a number of themes emerge. Firstly, the council has proven to be innovative regarding working methods (usually via the initiative of an elected member or either France or the United Kingdom). It has been shown that the low creep of politicization and diminishing returns frequently scuttles new working methods. Secondly, due to the constant turnover of members (five members replaced every year) and diplomatic staff, methods frequently come in and out of vogue. Thirdly, in recent times, the council has been closed to experimentation. Fewer innovations have been successfully mounted. Finally, a major grievance is the complete lack of interactivity in meetings—both public debates and informal consultations of the whole. Despite the listed impediments, working methods remain the most fertile ground for reform.

Notes

1 Loraine Sievers and Sam Daws, *The Procedure of the UN Security Council* (Oxford: Oxford University Press, 2014), 12.
2 UN Charter, Chapter V, Article 30.
3 Security Council Report, *Special Research Report No. 3: Security Council Transparency, Legitimacy and Effectiveness,* 2007. http://www.secur itycouncilreport.org/atf/cf/%7B65BFCF9B-6D27-4E9C-8CD3-CF6E4FF96FF 9%7D/Research%20Report_Working%20Methods%2018%20Oct%2007.pdf.
4 Edward C. Luck, *UN Security Council: Practice and Promise* (Abingdon: Routledge, 2006), 122.
5 Gary Quinlan, *Security Council Working Methods: Statement by HE Mr Gary Quinlan, Ambassador and Permanent Representative of Australia to the United Nations,* 2013. https://australia-unsc.gov.au/2013/10/secur ity-council-working-methods-2/.
6 *Note by the President of the Security Council* (Security Council S/2006/507) 19 July 2006, para. 1.
7 Security Council Report, *Special Research Report No. 1: Security Council Working Methods – A Work in Progress?* 2010. http://www.securitycouncilrep ort.org/atf/cf/%7B65BFCF9B-6D27-4E9C-8CD3-CF6E4FF96FF9%7D/Re search%20Report%20Working%20Methods%202010.pdf.
8 *Note by the President of the Security Council* (Security Council S/2006/507) 19 July 2006.
9 *Note by the President of the Security Council* (Security Council S/2006/507).
10 *Note by the President of the Security Council* (Security Council S/2006/507).
11 *Note by the President of the Security Council* (Security Council S/2006/507).

12 Austria, Chile, Costa Rica, Estonia, Finland, Gabon, Ghana, Hungary, Ireland, Jordan, Liechtenstein, Maldives, New Zealand, Norway, Papua New Guinea, Peru, Portugal, Saudi Arabia, Slovenia, Sweden, Switzerland, Tanzania, and Uruguay.

13 Volker Lehmann, *Reforming the Working Methods of the UN Security Council: The Next ACT* (New York: Friedrich-Ebert-Stiftung, 2013), 4.

14 Ratih Indraswari, "Reforming the UN Security Council," *Jakarta Post*, 17 December 2013. http://www.thejakartapost.com/news/2013/12/17/reform ing-un-security-council.html.

15 The Provisional Rule of Procedure of the UN Security Council, Rule 48.

16 David Bosco, *Five to Rule Them All: The UN Security Council and the Making of the Modern World* (New York: Oxford University Press, 2009).

17 UN Security Council, *Resolutions and Decisions of the Security Council, Volumes 37–46* (New York: United Nations, 2006), 277.

18 *No exit without strategy: Security Council decision-making and the closure or transition of United Nations peacekeeping operations* (S/2001/394), 20 April 2001.

19 *Statement by Ambassador Antonio Monteiro Permanent Representative of Portugal to the Fifty-Second Session of the General Assembly*, October 28, 1997.

20 Sievers and Daws, *The Procedure of the UN Security Council*, 10.

21 Anonymous Interviewee, Interview with Author, June 2011.

22 Security Council Report, *Security Council Working Methods: A Tale of Two Councils?*, 2015. http://www.securitycouncilreport.org/atf/cf/%7B65BF CF9B-6D27-4E9C-8CD3-CF6E4FF96FF9%7D/special_research_report__ working_methods_2014.pdf.

23 *Letter dated 3 July 2000 from the Permanent Representative of Bangladesh to the United Nations addressed to the Secretary-General* (Security Council S/2000/670), 31 July 2000, 8.

24 *Letter dated 3 July 2000 from the Permanent Representative of Bangladesh to the United Nations addressed to the Secretary-General* (Security Council S/2000/670).

25 Sievers and Daws, *The Procedure of the UN Security Council*, 54.

26 Sievers and Daws, *The Procedure of the UN Security Council*, 54.

27 Sievers and Daws, *The Procedure of the UN Security Council*, 55.

28 Sievers and Daws, *The Procedure of the UN Security Council*, 51, citing (A/49/667 – S/1994/1279).

29 Statement of the President of the Security Council (S/PRST/1994/81), 16 December 1994.

30 Statement of the President of the Security Council (S/PRST/1994/81).

31 UN Charter, Chapter VII, Article 44: "… invite that Member, if the Member so desires, to participate in the decisions of the Security Council concerning the employment of contingents of that Member's armed forces."

32 Security Council Report 2015, Security Council Working Methods: A tale of two Councils? http://www.securitycouncilreport.org/atf/cf/%7B65BFCF9 B-6D27-4E9C-8CD3-CF6E4FF96FF9%7D/special_research_report__work ing_methods_2014.pdf.

33 Security Council resolution 1353, 13 June 2001.

34 Resolution 2083 (2013), Presidential Statements S/PRST/2001/3, S/PRST/ 2002/56 and S/PRST/2009/24.

35 *Report of the Panel on United Nations Peace Operations* (Security Council [S/2000/809] and General Assembly [A/55/305]), 21 August 2001, 54.
36 *Report of the Panel on United Nations Peace Operations* (Security Council [S/2000/809] and General Assembly [A/55/305]), 21 August 2001, 54.
37 Security Council resolution 1353, 13 June 2001, Annex II, A (1).
38 Security Council resolution 1353, 13 June 2001, Annex II, A (1), para. 5 (b).
39 Security Council Report, *Security Council Working Methods: A Tale of Two Councils?*
40 United Nations Secretariat, *Background Note on the "Arria-Formula" Meetings of the Security Council Members*, 2002. http://www.un.org/en/sc/about/methods/bgarriaformula.shtml.
41 *Situation in Darfur, Sudan: Warrant of Arrest for Omar Hussan Ahmad Al Bashir* (International Criminal Court ICC-02/05–01/09), 9 March 2009.
42 Security Council Report, *Informal Interactive Dialogue*, 2015. http://www.securitycouncilreport.org/un-security-council-working-methods/atf/cf/%7B6 5BFCF9B-6D27-4E9C-8CD3-CF6E4FF96FF9%7D/working_methods_informal_interactive_dialogues.pdf.
43 Security Council Report, *Informal Interactive Dialogue*.
44 UN Charter, Chapter I, Article 1.
45 Small Arms and Light Weapons (SALW), Women Peace and Security, Security Sector Reform (SSR), Climate Change, Children and Conflict, Protection of Civilians (PoC), and Police.
46 Anonymous Interviewee, Interview with Author, June 2011.
47 Security Council Report, *Security Council Working Methods – A Work IN Progress?*
48 Anonymous Interviewee, Interview with Author, June 2011.
49 Anonymous Interviewee, Interview with Author, June 2011.
50 Security Council Report, *Penholders and Chairs*, 2015. http://www.securitycouncilreport.org/un-security-council-working-methods/pen-holders-and-chairs.php.
51 Security Council Report, *Penholders and Chairs*.
52 UN Charter, Chapter VI, Article 29.
53 UN Charter, Chapter VII, Article 43 (1).
54 UN Charter, Chapter VII, Article 47 (3).
55 Sievers and Daws, *The Procedure of the UN Security Council*, 472.
56 International Commission on Intervention and State Sovereignty, *The Responsibility to Protect: Report of the International Commission on Intervention and State Sovereignty* (Ottawa: The International Development Research Centre, 2001), XIII.
57 Laurent Fabius, "A Call for Self-Restraint at the U.N.," *New York Times*, 4 October 2013. http://www.nytimes.com/2013/10/04/opinion/a-call-for-self-restraint-at-the-un.html?_r=0.
58 Gareth Evans, *The French Veto Restraint Proposal: Making it work*, 2015. http://www.globalr2p.org/media/files/vetorestraintparis21jan25i15rev.pdf.
59 Laurent Fabius, "A Call for Self-Restraint at the U.N."
60 Stewart Patrick, "Limiting the veto in cases of mass atrocities: Is the proposed code of conduct workable?" 2013. http://www.cfr.org/france/limiting-veto-cases-mass-atrocities-proposed-code-conduct-workable/p36019.

6 The future of the debate and possibilities for reform

- The prospects for reform
- Compromise model: E-17
- Instruments of the council
- Enlivening meetings
- Conclusion

This volume works from the premise that reform is about "altering [an institution] for the better."[1] Put simply, if the council is defective, reforms should repair defects. The proposed reforms, outlined in the two preceding chapters, possess their own particular logic and emerge from a particular set of interests. This chapter is more prescriptive in nature, and centers on the chapter's key question: what reforms, not yet considered, might markedly enhance the agency of the council? The chapter will put forward a number of outside the box proposals. Since the early 90s, the UN has depended, for better or for worst, on peacekeeping and sanctions. With the council's penchant for peacekeeping and sanctions unlikely to decline, this chapter argues that perhaps it might be necessary to recast the reform debate to ensure that both peacekeeping operations and sanctions committees are adequately addressed.

The prospects for reform

Much like open debate within the council itself, the debate on reform has become inflexible and repetitious. Any current assessment of the debate would conclude that reform is less about reform, and more about playing a game of musical chairs. In other words, the membership is focused almost entirely on seats. A compromise is always a possibility. However, if any compromise is to be reached, members must abandon their maximalist positions and move towards the center.

In short, each must moderate their position. As of yet, the membership as a whole has not made "a commitment to undertaking robust negotiations, involving active give and take."[2] A compromise model or an intermediate arrangement might work to unify the positions of the various groups if undertaken in a spirit of compromise. At the same time, any compromise model should adhere to the principles of reform laid down in this study: namely enhanced council agency. It may seem factitious, but the reform debate should focus on reform. So far, much of the debate has been conducted in a vacuum, disconnected from questions of validity. What seems to have been forgotten is the fundamental scientific precept: mooted or hypothesized performance gains must be tested, and not simply taken at face value.

New permanency is a highly fraught proposition and one whose underlying assumptions are highly questionable. This volume has sought to unpack the proposition and question its underlying assumptions. In sum, the case for new permanency, prefaced on the representativeness equates to legitimacy argument, is tenuous. Furthermore, a model that does not accommodate the profound shifts that are to come is a sorely limited option, both now and at any time in the future. On balance, renewable seats are the better of the two options, because renewability is a proposition more malleable and accommodating of future realities. The benefits of renewability extend beyond mere future-proofing. The accountability mechanisms inherent (i.e. elections) to renewable seats give them an air of democratic respectability. The membership should recognize that expansion under either formula— renewability and new permanency—will involve the creation of a third category of membership, unless new permanent members are provided immediate and unconditional access to the veto power.

In theory, member-states should openly concede and accept the limitations of expansion: it is not a game changer. As this volume has reasoned, the addition of a host of new members or the addition of certain members (India, Brazil, Germany, Japan, South Africa, or Nigeria) will not radically transform the council's performance. Nevertheless, the reform debate has consumed far too much time and energy for member-states to abandon their fixation on composition and membership. The inequity argument has been repeated so often that many member-states have internalized the claim. They simply will not be convinced of the merits of any competing claim. For this reason, the council will need to cede ground to the call of the expansionists. The membership should not, however, wantonly sacrifice efficiency in the rush to allocate seats.

Compromise model: E-17

An intermediate or compromise model, based on the concept of renewability, is the only way forward. The use of the term intermediate suggests, such a model would lie somewhere in-between the current format and an envisaged future format. The potential compromise or intermediate reform options (A/B/C) presented below are attempts at expressing the principles of efficiency, regional balance, practicality, and accountability. In all, the model encompasses a range of potential configurations depending on the whims of the membership. The basic model slates a modest increase to 22 seats: the current five permanent seats (P-5) and an elected seventeen (E-17).

Option A

The most contentious element of Option A is a radical reorganization of the electoral groupings. The proposed reconfiguration is radical because it effects not only the elections of the Security Council, but also the elections in other UN fora. The overall aim of the reconfiguration is to strengthen proportional representation (see Table 6.1). As a general rule of thumb, elected seats would be allocated on the basis of one elected seat for every 10 electoral group members (1:10 formula). Expanding some electoral groups, creating new ones, and reducing the membership of others strengthens the cohesiveness of the

Table 6.1 Proportional representation of option A

Grouping	No. Group members	Elected seats	% of total UN membership	% of elected seats	Members per elected seat
Europe	35	2	18%	11.7%	16.5
Eastern Europe	12	1	6.2%	5.8%	11
Americas and the Caribbean	35	3	18%	17.6%	11.3
South/Central Asia	13	2	6.7%	11.7%	6.5
Asia-Pacific	30	3	15.5%	17.6%	10
Middle East	14	1	7.3%	5.9%	14
Africa	54	5	28%	29.4%	10.8
	193	**17**			

entire electoral system. Individual electoral groups would be granted the flexibly to informally determine which seats might be designated short-term seats and/or up to seven long-term seats.

- **Europe:** A new European group would be created from the shell of the WEOG group. The group would retain WEOG's two elected seats, but would be expanded from 28 to 35 members. The expansion would include all 28 members of the EU, as well as all non-EU countries in Western and Northern Europe. The group's permanent members would be France and the UK.
- **Eastern Europe:** Because of the reconfiguration of WEOG, the Eastern Europe group would be reduced in size, with 11 members vying for a solidary elected seat on the council. The group's permanent member would be Russia.
- **The Americas and the Caribbean:** The GRULAC group would be granted three elected seats, and expanded to include Canada and the US. The membership of the new Americas and Caribbean Group would be an overlay of the membership of 35-member Organization of American States (OAS). The group may choose to informally allocate elected seats on a regional basis: one each to Central America and North America (Cuba, Mexico, Canada, Belize, Costa Rica, El Salvador, Guatemala, Honduras, Nicaragua, and Panama), CARICOM, and Latin America. The group's permanent member would be the United States.
- **Central and South Asia:** The Asia-Pacific group include the sub-continental or South Asian countries (India, Pakistan, Sri Lanka, Nepal, Bangladesh, Bhutan, and the Maldives) and the former Soviet states of Central Asian (Kazakhstan, Kyrgyzstan, Tajikistan, Turkmenistan, and Uzbekistan). The allocation of two seats is in anticipation of India holding one of the seats for an extended period.
- **Asia-Pacific:** The new Asia-Pacific group would include ASEAN (Association of Southeast Asian Nations) countries, the Pacific Island Forum (including Australia and New Zealand), and countries of Northeast Asia (Mongolia, Japan, China, DPRK, and the Republic of Korea). The group would be granted three elected seats. The group's permanent member would be China.
- **Middle East:** At present, the Middle East is situated in the Asia-Pacific group. A nation from the Arab world is always present on the council, whether North African or Middle Eastern. The new Middle East group of 13 members would be granted one elected seat.
- **Africa:** The Africa group would remain untouched in the reconfiguration, but would receive five electoral seats. Formally dividing

the bloc is problematic. Firstly, if the groups were designated on the basis of UN's sub-regions, some would be considerably larger than others. A West Africa group might include a possible 17 members, while a North Africa group might only include six. The group may choose to allocate the five seats using any formula they see fit, perhaps allocating three short-term seats and two long-term seats.

Option B

Option B proposes a minor reconfiguration of the electoral group system. This most logical reform would alter the membership of both European groups (see Table 6.3). As proposed in option A, the European group includes all 28 members European Union (EU) members. At present, 11 members of the EU are also members of the EEG. In 2006 to 2007, a third of the Security Council were also EU members (France, United Kingdom, Slovenia, and Denmark and Greece in 2006, and Belgium). Clearly, this scenario should not be repeated. A reorganized WEOG (renamed Europe + five) would consist of 28 EU members plus 12 others states (Australia, Israel, Canada, US, New Zealand, Turkey and seven non-EU states). This would create a 41-member Europe + five group and a smaller 12 member EEG.

Under this option, the allocation of seats would be follow the 1:10 formula guide proposed in option A. Five seats allocated to the larger Asia-Pacific and Africa blocs, three each for Europe and GRULAC, and one for the EEG (see Table 6.4). Under Option B the new Europe + five group would be allocated three elected seats. Selection of this option would bring the system into approximate proportional balance.

Option C

The third proposed option retains the five current electoral groups, while the 1:10 formula is once again applied to determine the possible allocation of seats. Under Option C, WEOG would be allocated two elected seats; Asia-Pacific would be granted five; the Africa group would have a total of five seats; GRULAC would receive three; and EEG would receive two seats. The introduction of informal rules, like those that governs the allocation of the Arab seat could ensure flexibility and a degree of balance within some of the groups. In the EEG, the allocation of seats might follow an informal rule: 11 Eastern European EU member-states for one seat, the other 11 EEG members for the other. In WEOG, one seat might be a long-term seat, one for a non-EU member or other state, and the remaining seat allocated to a Western

Table 6.2 Membership of the seven electoral groups (option A)

Electoral Group	Members
Europe 35 members	Andorra, Austria, Belgium, Bulgaria, Croatia, Cyprus, Czech Republic, Denmark, Estonia, Finland, **France**, Germany, Greece, Hungary, Iceland, Ireland, Italy, Latvia, Liechtenstein, Lithuania, Luxembourg, Malta, Monaco, Netherlands, Norway, Poland, Portugal, Romania, San Marino, Slovakia, Slovenia, Switzerland, Spain, Sweden, and the **United Kingdom**
Eastern Europe 12 members	Albania, Armenia, Azerbaijan, Belarus, Bosnia and Herzegovina, Georgia, Macedonia, Moldova, Montenegro, **Russia**, Serbia, and Ukraine
The Americas and the Caribbean 35 Members	Antigua and Barbuda, Argentina, Bahamas, Barbados, Belize, Bolivia, Brazil, Canada, Chile, Colombia, Costa Rica, Cuba, Dominica, Dominican Republic, Ecuador, El Salvador, Grenada, Guatemala, Guyana, Haiti, Honduras, Jamaica, Mexico, Nicaragua, Panama, Paraguay, Peru, Saint Kitts and Nevis, Saint Lucia, Saint Vincent and the Grenadines, Suriname, Trinidad and Tobago, the **United States**, Uruguay, and Venezuela.
South and Central Asia 13 members	Afghanistan, Bangladesh, Bhutan, India, Kazakhstan, Kyrgyzstan, Maldives, Nepal, Pakistan, Sri Lanka, Tajikistan, Turkmenistan, and Uzbekistan
Asia-Pacific 30 members	Australia, Brunei, Cambodia, China, Democratic People's Republic of Korea, Fiji, Indonesia, Japan, Kiribati, Laos, Malaysia, Marshall Islands, Micronesia, Mongolia, Myanmar, Nauru, New Zealand, Palau, Papua New Guinea, Philippines, Republic of Korea, Samoa, Singapore, Solomon Islands, Thailand, Timor-Leste, Tonga, Tuvalu, Vanuatu, and Vietnam
Middle East 14 members	Bahrain, Iraq, Iran, Israel, Jordan, Kuwait, Lebanon, Oman, Qatar, Saudi Arabia, Syria, Turkey, United Arab Emirates (UAE), and Yemen
Africa 54 members	African Union + Morocco

Table 6.3 Membership list for the two reconfigured electoral groups (option B)

Electoral Group	Members
Europe + 6 41 members	Australia (o), Andorra, Austria, Belgium, Bulgaria, Canada (o), Croatia, Cyprus, Czech Republic, Denmark, Estonia, Finland, **France**, Germany, Greece, Hungary, Iceland, Israel (o), Ireland, Italy, Latvia, Liechtenstein, Lithuania, Luxembourg, Malta, Monaco, Netherlands, New Zealand (o), Norway, Poland, Portugal, Romania, San Marino, Slovakia, Slovenia, Switzerland, Spain, Sweden, Turkey (o), the **United Kingdom**, and the **United States (o)**
Eastern Europe 12 members	Albania, Armenia, Azerbaijan, Belarus, Bosnia and Herzegovina, Georgia, Macedonia, Moldova, Montenegro, **Russia**, Serbia, and Ukraine

Table 6.4 Proportional representation (option B)

Grouping	No. Group members	Elected seats	% of total UN membership	% of elected seats	Members per elected seat
Europe +6	41	3	21.7%	17.6%	12.3
EEG	12	1	6.2%	5.8%	12
GRULAC	33	3	17.1%	17.6%	11
Asia-Pacific	53	5	27.5%	29.5%	10.6
Africa	54	5	28%	29.5%	10.8
	193	**17**			

European EU member-state. The Africa Group already elects members to the council on the basis of informal sub-regional representation. An expanded council with five elected seats for Africa might informally reflect the regional balance of the AU Peace and Security Council: North Africa, Southern Africa, West Africa, African Great Lakes, and Central Africa.

A stepping-stone?

The following section lays out a potential decision tree. The first stage of the step-by-step approach would require the membership reaching a compromise on the composition of the new council, either by pursing a host of options currently on the table or developing another. In order to achieve compromise, it is likely that the membership will need to

Table 6.5 Proportional representation (option C)

Grouping	No. Group members	Elected seats	% of total UN membership	% of elected seats	Members per elected seat
WEOG	28	2	14.5%	11.7%	14
EEG	23	2	12%	11.7%	11.5
GRULAC	33	3	17.1%	17.6%	11
Asia-Pacific	54	5	28%	29.5%	10.8
Africa	54	5	28%	29.5%	10.8
	192	**17**			

adopt an intermediate model, a stepping stone to a future council. The search for an intermediate model would not mean a victory for the UfC, as such, nor would it precipitate a G4 concession. The G4 would have to abandon their aspirations, at least in the short term. The intermediate model could be marketed to the G4 as a stepping stone to permanency. At this point in time, the choice for the G4 is rather stark. The immediate option means accepting a seat on the council that might lead to a future permanency, while the status quo means no seat now, and a rather dim prospect of a future permanent seat. The UfC would also have to embrace a longer-term renewable option, and abandon its current limited renewability option. The UfC would need to concede to accepting new permanency, if the membership so chooses (after the interim period). The C-10 would have to redraft a new consensus to replace the Ezulwini Consensus. A new African-regional consensus would forgo the option of permanency with veto in favor of an agreed upon intermediate renewable option.

The beauty of an intermediate model is that it would allow aspirant members to audition for permanent seats. Following the interim period, if the membership chose to reject the bids of the aspirants, then the renewable seats would remain, in perpetuity. To ensure the viability of the compromise, the membership would need to commit to holding an Article 109 conference for the purpose of reviewing the present charter (with special consideration paid to Chapter V of the charter) after a predetermined interim period. As for the length of this period, 12 years would be optimal. After which, members would have garnered sufficient information to assess the performance of the council and that of the long-serving elected members.

In order to create an intermediate council, the membership would need to choose between two avenues in regards to renewability. The first option would see all elected seats made renewable. That is, retiring members would be immediately eligible for re-election (after completing their two-year terms). Amendment of the charter would only require the deletion of one word: "not" from Article 23 (2). Instead, the last line of an amended Article 23 (2) would read "a retiring member shall be eligible for immediate re-election." Formally and technically, all 17 seats would be renewable, however.

Secondly, the membership might choose to create a third category of membership with long-term renewable seats (four-year renewable). Under all three of the options presented above (Options A/B/C), up to seven of the elected seats could be converted to long-term renewable seats (four-year terms), while the remaining 10 would operate as short-term elected seats. The downside of locking in a particular structure is that it limits future options.

In the first round of the process, three amendments to the charter would be required, depending on the choices made. Article 23 (1) would be amended, replacing "fifteen" with the total number decided upon (+20). A second amendment would alter Article 23 (2) to accommodate the new category (or instate renewability), while Article 27 (2) and (3) would need to be amended to modify the super majority (two-thirds) required when voting. An additional number of amendments could be made to clean up obsolete sections of the charter: the deletion of the enemy clauses (Articles 53, 77, and 107), the deletion of the USSR and the Republic of China, and the insertion of their replacements, the Russian Federation and the People's Republic of China.

The membership would then begin the process of deciding whether or not to commit to the next stage of the reform process—the election of permanent members. There can never be an ironclad guarantee of second-stage reform, however. The second stage of the process would require three charter amendments. The first would involve the deletion of those sections of Article 27 (2) that relate to renewable seats (amended 12 years prior). A second would alter Article 23 (1) to include the names of the new permanent members. If the new permanent members were not granted veto, then Article 27 (3) would need to be reworded to reflect the difference in status: "including the concurring votes of the Russian Federation, the People's Republic of China, France, the United Kingdom, and the United States of America."

A strategy for compromise

Would-be reformers should seek out opportunities to experiment. There are no simple solutions to the current impasse, however. It would seem that the formality of the IGN continues to work to reinforce the impasse. An informal external process that bridges divides will therefore need to be developed. A small, informal cross-grouping committee comprised UfC, G4, L-69, C-10, and Arab Group members might be a multi-partisan approach to developing an intermediate model, if the participants are prepared to moderate their positions and meet in a spirit of compromise. This group might seek to develop a working document—a suggestion of Gowan and Gordon:

> Initial discussions on the idea of the working document should be conducted in informal retreats or conferences to take stock of member state perspectives on the possibilities, and explore creative approaches with the input of experts from civil society and academia.[3]

Once a workable consensus is built, then the IGN can lock in the informal agreement and drive the formal process. A holistic approach tailored to engage regions, capitals, and permanent missions in New York, supported by civil society and academia, might be another potential experiment. Currently, the debate is beset by inertia, the result of frustration, disinterest, and pessimism.[4] In fact, downcast pronouncements, speaking of the utter hopelessness of the situation, only serve to reinforce the inertia around the debate.

In many capitals of the world, Security Council reform does not rate too highly on the agendas of policy and decision-makers. To address the deficit in attention, reformists must focus their attention on building a constituency for reform. Foreign policy think tanks, civil society, academia, thought leaders, and public intellectuals can lead the conversations. After more than 20 years of debate reform fatigue has well and truly set in. A critical mass is required to break the inertia, and spur members into action. Here civil society has a role to play. Yet, few think tanks, academics, UN associations, or NGOs appear interested in applying their leverage to help break the deadlock and encourage meaningful conversations on reform.

Once a strong and influential constituency is mobilized, then civil society can openly engage governments and question their inflexibility on the issue. Gowan and Gordon have recommended the appointment of a special envoy or high level panel (HLP) to "help bridge the disconnection between UNHQ and member state capitals through building awareness, interest, and activity around the issue of UNSC reform."[5] An experienced and charismatic former statesperson would be a prime candidate for the position of envoy. She or he would have to embrace a form of shuttle diplomacy; traveling from capital to capital (including regional hubs) brokering dialogues, sounding out positions, encouraging compromise, and conducting outreach events through the constituency-builders mentioned above.

In Addis Ababa, a number of decisions need to be made regarding the African consensus on reform. As mentioned above, the Ezulwini Consensus must be re-forged. The African bloc, with its 54 members, is the largest single group in the debate. Hence, a shift in position or a relaxation of certain stipulations would almost certainly precipitate a shift across the board. Firstly, if "Africa is opposed in principle to the veto,"[6] as the Consensus makes clear, then the African bloc must abandon its "common justice"[7] position on the veto, which would see all permanent members granted veto rights (see Appendix II, this volume). Common justice aside, new permanency coupled with veto extension would be a disaster for the council's credibility—which is not in the best interests of Africa, as a whole. Secondly, the African common position needs to accept the competing claims of the big five—Ethiopia, Egypt, Algeria, South Africa, and Nigeria—all of whom are vying for the two hypothetical permanent seats. Currently, Nigeria is the frontrunner for a permanent seat, but there is no clear-cut number two candidate among the other four. Furthermore, the election of two powers would be to the exclusion of the other three. The result: a bitterly divided Africa. This conundrum only serves to illustrate the advantages of renewability and its capacity to accommodate change.

Instruments of the council

First, the council must be made more capable of wielding the instruments at its disposal. Second, the instruments themselves need to be made more incisive. Third, the toolbox itself needs to be enlarged by way of innovation.

Peace operations

It cannot be denied: the council has a penchant for peace operations. In 17 years, the council has deployed over 65 missions to Africa, the Middle East, Southeast Asia, Central and South Asia, Europe, Central America, and the Caribbean. The parameters of deployment need to be altered to ensure missions are placed on the surest of footings. From the outset, the council must be more contemplative and more prepared to pose the obvious but difficult questions: Is this mandate achievable? Are our ambitions conflated? By authorizing this mission, are we setting it up for failure? The playbook containing the council's templates and its overarching interventionist paradigms should come under scrutiny. The council should always question the reigning paradigmatic tendencies, which guide its responses. The council needs to more readily ponder looming decisions, rather than rush them. Poor or rushed decisions, made before the facts are truly understood, can railroad responses (path dependency) and may even set a mission down the path to failure.

Likewise, wish-list mandates burden missions with responsibilities that they are ill equipped to carry out. Instead, the council must look at adopting incremental, pragmatic and flexible approaches born of a close reading of the facts on ground and the core political realities. The two-staged mandating process mooted in Brahimi is one experiment worth considering. Such a process would allow for a more vivid information picture to be drawn prior to the adoption of each mandate. This in turn allows for a more careful assessment of means and ends, and a more precisely contextualized mandate. Reflecting on the High Level Independent Panel on Peace Operations, Jean Arnault summarizes the recommendation:

> It means a transformation of the mandating process, better adjusted to the reality of continuously evolving political and military situations. It also means a transformation of the budget process at the UN, which currently favors front-loading mission tasks and resources rather than allowing for ongoing re-adjustment of mission mandates depending on context.[8]

The council is regularly accused of deploying missions into strategic and security vacuums. The council must learn to moderate its peacekeeping habit, especially in circumstances of limited political will, resources, and leadership. If it is to deploy, then the council needs to develop a sense of strategic vision. This may seem utopian and wholly unrealistic, but it is a completely necessary recommendation. As this volume has suggested, the council needs to be flexible in composition, deliberation, thinking, and implementation. It needs to learn how to better deal with the unexpected, anticipate changing situations, and guard against false assumptions. In other words, the council needs an imagination. The council cannot, however, strategize along rigid, unbending, predetermined trajectories in the pursuit of a desired state of affairs. Lawrence Freeman, in his weighty tome *Strategy: A History,* expounds on the fundamental nature of the strategic mindset:

Strategy therefore starts with an existing state of affairs and only gains meaning by an awareness of how, for better or worse, it could be different ... the starting point will still be the challenges of the present rather than the promise of the future. With each move from one state of affairs to another, the combination of ends and means will be reappraised.[9]

Reappraisal is a vital element of strategy-making. Council-mandated periodic or episodic reviews should be undertaken to identify opportunities and challenges. These reviews should not be sanitized reports. Instead they should tell the council "what it needs to know, not what it wants to hear."[10] A non-exhaustive list of framing questions is laid out below:

- Is the mission confounded by its circumstances? If yes, what fundamental maladies exist and how can they be rectified?
- Are troop contributors genuinely committed to the mission, and do they understand what the council is expects of their troops (vis-à-vis the use of force)?
- Are the mission's programs adequately supported (i.e. SSR, DDR, and other reform programs)?
- Has the political situation evolved? Does the council need to adjust its approach and political overtures?
- Is the peace or the mission itself threatened by spoilers? How can the mission better contend with these challenges without prejudice?

Sanctions

Sanctions have remained a favorite tool of the council since the end of the Cold War. Despite their popularity, sanctions have remained problematic. They are easy and inexpensive for the council to impose. With a stroke of a pen, an arms embargo can be imposed or a series of targeted measures brought to bear on a non-compliant rebel leader. Monitoring and enforcing UN sanctions is much harder and costlier. For every stringent, tightly regulated sanctions regime (such as Iran or North Korea), there are half a dozen poorly enforced regimes. The majority of sanctions regimes are not backed by credible independent enforcement capabilities—a monitoring taskforce. Instead, the council relies on member-states to do their utmost to administer the regimes that it has imposed. In general, the problem is one of will and capacity. Some member-states lack the will to expend resources to enforce or tighten sanctions regimes; their willingness might be born of indifference or a repudiation of a sanctions edict. Others might possess the will, but they may simply lack the capacity to adequately carry sanctions into effect.

The effectiveness of sanctions cannot be assessed using a simple binary equation: the conflict stopped or the targeted actor complied, therefore the sanctions were a success—correlation does not imply causation. Sanctions are arguably most effective as a signaling device rather than a means of direct coercion. Sanctions stigmatize those targeted. They are imposed with the hope of positively altering a government or armed group's internal dynamics. Sanctions also fulfill a useful purpose more broadly—the do something strategy. They signal to the broader international community that the council is doing something about the situation. More careful attention should be paid to how sanctions interact with and reinforce other measures (i.e. how does this sanctions regime affect mediation efforts?)

The subsidiary body format could be radically overhauled using a model adopted by the Peacebuilding Commission (PBC) known as the country-specific configuration. Sanctions committees would need to include the permanent members of the council, but could be chaired by an elected member (as is current practice). The designated chair could also act as the co-penholder on the file. Non-council members might be selected on the basis of their importance vis-à-vis implementation: including neighboring countries, key trading partners, and regional powers. The selection of non-council members would be an unavoidably political activity, requiring a resolution of the council.

Including non-council members on sanctions committees might not only reduce the deliberative deficit, but also improve the implementation of sanctions regimes. The inclusion of potentially belligerent or unhelpful member-states on committees might be a necessity in certain cases. Allowing such members access to the committee, but limiting their ability to subvert committee processes would be critical. This would require a change in the voting rules of sanctions committees, which currently work on the basis of unanimity. In the end, the committee may be required to confront these members. It can be argued that including rather than excluding certain member-states on this basis could lend legitimacy to the process.

Enlivening meetings

Meetings of the council are riddled with a lack of interactivity. The problem affects not only public meetings, but also informal consultations. Members have internalized a style of operating which is

characterized as pro forma and ritualistic. Healthier and more meaningful exchanges, driven not by a contestation of interests, but by a
contestation of ideas, would almost certainly garner higher quality
outcomes. How can this be achieved?

Member-states can take the initiative. A friendly but forthright aide-
mémoire should be issued to council members reminding each of their
responsibilities vis-à-vis the maintenance of international peace and
security. Continual blocking and unruly politicization of areas of the
agenda, that were once permissible, limits the agency of the council. If
enough council and non-council members chant reminders of positive
past practice and the negative credibility implications that result from
politicization on the margins, then powerful states may change their calculations and behaviors. This might be naïve, but it is a necessary suggestion for the restoration of the council. The president of the council
can take also the initiative. Outside of thematic practices, the presidents of the council have "become more restrained (or constrained)
when making statements to the media at the press stakeout."[11] As the
chairs of all meetings, the presidents hold more power than they realize.

The UN secretary-general can take the initiative. The secretary-general
should consider enlivening affairs through invocation of article 99.
Initially, the secretary-general would need to exercise both caution and
prudence. However, once members learn to accept Article 99 interventions,
then the exercise becomes a commonplace practice.

Conclusion

The prospects for reform of the size and composition are decidedly
poor. The blocs have fortified their positions and appear intent on
fighting it out through the IGN, which is heading into its eighth year
under its second chair. This chapter has made a number of suggestions
aimed at breaking the impasse, none of which are particularly revolu-
tionary. All require a genuinely receptive membership. If the membership
truly desires reform, the need for compromise is paramount. A two-thirds
consensus simply cannot be built by any other means. A compromise
model is the only option, not a compromised model.

Notes

1 Oxford English Dictionary, Definition of "Reform," (Oxford: Oxford
  University Press, 2013).
2 Zahir Tanin, *Letter of the Chair of the Intergovernmental Negotiations on
  the question of equitable representation on the increase in membership of the*

Security Council and related matters, 2012. http://www.un.org/en/ga/presi dent/66/Letters/PDF/Security%20Council%20Reform-PGA%20letter%2027 %20July.pdf.

3 Richard Gowan and Nora Gordon, *Pathways to Security Council Reform* (New York: New York University Center on International Cooperation, May 2014), 28.

4 Gowan and Gordon, *Pathways to Security Council Reform*, 5.

5 Gowan and Gordon, *Pathways to Security Council Reform*, 23.

6 See Appendix 2, this volume.

7 See Appendix 2, this volume.

8 Jean Arnault, *A Background to the Report of the High-Level Panel on Peace Operations*, 2015. http://peaceoperationsreview.org/thematic-essays/a -background-to-the-report-of-the-high-level-panel-on-peace-operations/.

9 Lawrence Freedman, *Strategy: A History* (New York: Oxford University Press, 2013), 611.

10 *Report of the Panel on United Nations Peace Operations*, (Security Council and General Assembly A/55/305 – S/2000/809), 21 August 2000.

11 Security Council Report, *Security Council Working Methods: A Tale of Two Councils?* 2015. http://www.securitycouncilreport.org/atf/cf/%7B65BFCF9B -6D27-4E9C-8CD3-CF6E4FF96FF9%7D/special_research_report__worki ng_methods_2014.pdf.

Conclusion

- **The case against new permanency**
- **Compromise**

The Chinese idiom "paper tiger" refers to something that is outwardly powerful, yet in reality is ineffective.[1] Many observers view the Security Council as the quintessential paper tiger—possessing limitless power, yet limited in the exercise of its power. The reform debate captures and channels this sentiment. The council is in trouble, the reformists argue, and in urgent need of repair. An expansion and an altering of the council's composition is the answer, they contend.

The prevailing wisdom, among some at the UN, proposes that if the right countries are present, then the good outcomes can be expected. This volume has railed against this superficial proposition. An alternative argument holds more weight—the composition of the council is not as important as its mechanics. As Ian Hurd has argued, "external change need not reduce the council's effectiveness even in the absence of formal change, as long as the informal practice of the council adapts to the new environment."[2]

The council inhabits a vastly different world that which it did in 1945–1946. Seventy years on, many would argue that the council has not adapted to twenty-first century realities. It is true that the number of seats has remained virtually unchanged. The council has, nevertheless, adapted to changing circumstances. In 1965, the number of elected seats was increased from six to 10. In 1972, the ROC was forced out of the council and the organization altogether, relinquishing its permanent seat to the PRC. In 1990, the USSR left its seat to the Russian Federation.

Faced with a complex and perplexing set of challenges thrown up in the wake of end of the Cold War, the council was forced to adapt. In dealing with the Iran-Iraq war, the horseshoe table was instilled with an instinct for innovation, which carried it forth into the twenty-first century. The council came to rely on a host of new and innovative practices. Peacekeeping was fundamentally reshaped, sanctions regimes made smarter, and the day-to-day methods of the council reformatted. The council has not stood still. Informally, it is has remained malleable and contemporary.

This volume has called the debate back to square one by asking the obvious, yet fundamental question, what is reform? How can the council be made more capable of fulfilling its mandate? To appreciate the potential of genuine reform, one must venture beyond the unitary equation: composition change equals reform. The concept of agency, presented in Chapter 2, provides an insight on the question of capacity, while avoiding the dilemmas of defining effectiveness. Agency is a mere explanation of a very complex picture of how the council works, and how it might work better.

First, the council must be more precise in the way it responds to conflict. Its approaches must be context-sensitive, close to the ground, yet regional in their breadth. The council in a word must be more contemplative. Second, members must guard against tunnel vision and path dependent responses; rather they should trust more pragmatic strategic decision making and the power of evaluative reappraisal. The council needs to learn the lessons of Iraq and Afghanistan and accept the limitations of external interventionism. The gap between ends and the means must be closed, either by investing more or limiting ambitions (i.e. Christmas tree mandates). Third, the P-5 and the other members of the council, in general, need to be more aware. Together they must make the most of "opportunities to be effective."[3] When opportunities present, leaders need to mobilize sufficient political will and resources to sustain efforts, break inertia, indifference, and crisis fatigue. There exists no reason why the council cannot achieve some higher level of effectiveness. The key, once again, is the membership. Ultimately, the council is only an institutional framework through which member-states operate in pursuit of common ends.

The case against new permanency

An argument can be made that the central frustration lying at the heart of the debate is the veto, and the inherent inequity that it creates. The veto is an anachronism. It was at first a justifiable anachronism, made defensible by the four-policemen concept and backed by considerable force of arms. The Cold War, however, put paid to the military staff committee and many of the articles of Chapter V and VII.

Hence, the initial justification for the veto, made on the basis of the five-policeman, quickly and almost completely evaporated. In the twenty-first century, the veto has come to be almost universally seen as a disproportionate power and an impediment to credible international action to crises The veto power might be an anachronism, but it is here to stay. The P-5 will never foreseeably forgo the power, at least formally.

This reality should be borne in mind when contemplating reform: perceptions of unjustified inequality damage the credibility of the institution.

The problem with new permanency is that it is symptomatic of the worst elements of old permanency. If the aspirant countries were installed as permanent members, then the membership at large would be condoning anachronism, lowest common denominator-ism, inefficiency, and potential paralysis. Granting six new permanent members the veto would be to embrace foolishness of the highest order; a blatant denial of the both the realities of today and yesterday. Plainly, additional vetoes would sorely limit the agency of the council in many parts of the world. The current impasse over Syria, which is so damaging to the council's credibility, could conceivably be replicated again and again in other parts of the world, depending on the interests at stake for the new permanent members.

Firstly, new permanency is not an exercise in democratization. Quite simply, the membership cannot hold permanent members accountable for their performance by any democratic means. Secondly, new permanency does not future-proof the council. It should be remembered that permanent is a long time. The powerful of today may not be the powerful of tomorrow. Inevitability, a new aspirant class will emerge with a claim to the high table. Thirdly, new permanency denies the actual nature of council agency, which relies more on diplomatic imagination as opposed to raw economic or military power. Finally, if new permanency is instituted and the power of veto not granted to the six or more new permanent members, then a new category of membership is de facto created: permanent members without veto.

Compromise

"The negotiations (IGN) are not negotiations … no one has the authority to negotiate,"[4] uttered one former permanent representative. The long and winding reform debate has produced various initiatives and openings—all have been non-starters—on account of tactical game playing and acrimony. Breaking the impasse and building a consensus could prove difficult, if not impossible. A membership of 193 is seemingly too vast a group of states to corral.

If the membership truly seeks reform, it must collectively seek out a compromise solution. The blocs and their key constituents must give up their maximalist positions in favour of the middle ground. In chapter 6 of this volume, a set of potential options for compromise were laid down.

The most radical of these options envisages a major revision of the electoral groups, encapsulating a few subtle alterations and the creation of smaller more inclusive groupings. Overlaying well-established pre-existing regional organizations and groups serves the council's regionalism agenda as well. Ultimately, even if the proposed groupings are deemed unsuitable, electoral group reconfiguration should still be considered as part of the reform debate. Aside from electoral group alteration, the model proposes a modest increase of seven seats: the creation of a 22-member council. The smaller the council, the more manageable and efficient it is, hence a more modest expansion. The smaller council is also amenable to the P-5—Russia and the US have both indicated a preference for a council in the low twenties. In proportional terms, the difference between a 22- and 25-member council is negligible—1.55 percent to be precise. Balance can be achieved through the careful and proportional allocation of seats. As the models and options presented in the previous chapter indicate, a reasonably fair and equitable balance can be struck.

For too long, the permanent membership has monopolized decision-making and colonized the working methods of the council. This is not to the benefit of the council's deliberative legitimacy. A more inclusive and consultative council is likely a more legitimate council, as the logic of legitimacy attests. The membership of the council needs to ensure its informal practices continue to adapt to the changing world; enlivening informal consultations, country-specific constellations for subsidiary bodies, and a greater diversity of penholders are all potential boxes to be ticked. An imaginative exploration of the possibilities for innovation should be encouraged, and experiments welcomed. Working methods recognized for their utility have to be informally codified, sharpened, and protected against curse of politicization. A smorgasbord of opportunities for reform exists beyond the fixation with expansion and composition.

Is it a case of reform or die for the Security Council? Reports of the death of the council have been greatly exaggerated. Its imperfections are well cited. The council will always be an undeniably human institution, weathered, but still eminently functional. It has endured, despite pronouncements to the contrary.

This book has expounded a cautionary tale. Ill-conceived reform could be the greatest false dawn in UN history: the burden of a large, unwieldy, and inefficient council, confounded by an enlarged clique, is not a desirable end state.

Notes

1 Paper Tiger, n.: A person, country, etc., that appears powerful or threatening but is actually weak or ineffective.
2 Ian Hurd, "Security Council Reform: Informal Membership and Practice," in *The Once and Future Security Council*, ed. Bruce Russett (New York: St Martin's, 1997), 137.
3 Anonymous Interviewee, Interview with Author, June 2011.
4 Anonymous Interviewee, Interview with Author, August 2015.

Appendix I
Vetos

US

1 The Middle East, including the Palestinian question

13 July 2006—*"Condemning* military assault being carried out by Israel, the occupying Power, in the Gaza Strip, which has caused the killing and injury of dozens of Palestinian civilians, and the destruction of Palestinian property and civilian infrastructure, notably Gaza's main power station, and condemning also the detention of democratically elected Palestinian and other officials" (S/2006/508 Preamble Clause 4).

2 The Middle East, including the Palestinian question

10 November 2006—*"Condemning* the military operations being carried out by Israel, the occupying Power, in the Gaza Strip, in particular the attack that took place in Beit Hanoun on 8 November 2006, which have caused loss of civilian life and extensive destruction of Palestinian property and vital infrastructure" (S/2006/878 Preamble Clause 4).

3 The Middle East, including the Palestinian question

5 October 2004—*"Condemning* the broad military incursion and attacks by the Israeli occupying forces in the area of Northern Gaza Strip, including in and around the Jabaliya refugee camp, resulting in extensive human casualties and destruction and exacerbating the dire humanitarian situation" (S/2004/783 Preamble Clause 3).

4 The Middle East, including the Palestinian question

24 March 2004—"*Condemns* the most recent extrajudicial execution committed by Israel, the occupying Power, that killed Sheikh Ahmed Yassin along with six other Palestinians outside a mosque in Gaza City and calls for a complete cessation of extrajudicial executions" (S/2004/240 Operative Clause 1).

5 The Middle East, including the Palestinian question

October 14, 2004- "*Decides* that the construction by Israel, the occupying Power, of a wall in the Occupied Territories departing from the armistice line of 1949 is illegal under relevant provisions of international law and must be ceased and reversed" (S/2003/980 Operative Clause 1).

6 The Middle East, including the Palestinian question

16 September 2003—"*Demands* that Israel, the occupying Power, desist from any act of deportation and cease any threat to the safety of the elected President of the Palestinian Authority" (S/2003/891 Operative Clause 2).

7 The Middle East, including the Palestinian question

19 December 2002—"*Expressing grave concern* at the killing by the Israeli occupying forces of several United Nations employees, including the recent killing of one international staff member in the Jenin refugee camp" (S/2002/1385 Preamble Clause 4).

8 Bosnia

30 June 2002—"*Decides* to extend the mandate of UNMIBH, which includes the IPTF, for an additional period terminating on 31 December 2002, and also decides that, during that period, the IPTF shall continue to be entrusted with the tasks set out in Annex 11 of the Peace Agreement, including the tasks referred to in the Conclusions of the London, Bonn, Luxembourg, Madrid and Brussels Conferences and agreed by the authorities in Bosnia and Herzegovina" (S/2002/1420 Operative Clause 19—Chapter VII).

9 The Middle East, including the Palestinian question

14 December 2001—"*Demands* the immediate cessation of all acts of violence, provocation and destruction, as well as the return to the

positions and arrangement which existed prior to September 2000" (S/ 2001/1199 Operative Clause 1).

10 The Middle East, including the Palestinian question

26 March 2001—"*Requests* the Secretary-General to consult the parties on immediate and substantive steps to implement this resolution and to report to the Council within one month of the adoption of this resolution and expresses the readiness of the Council to act upon receipt of the report to set up an appropriate mechanism to protect Palestinian civilians, including through the establishment of a United Nations observer force" (S/2001/270 Operative Clause 8).

11 The Middle East, including the Palestinian question

21 March 1997—"*Demands* that Israel immediately cease construction of the Jabal Abu Ghneim settlement in East Jerusalem, as well as all other Israeli settlement activities in the occupied territories" (SC/ 1997/ 241 Operative Clause 1).

12 The Middle East, including the Palestinian question

7 March 1997—"*Calls upon* the Israeli authorities to refrain from all actions or measures, including settlement activities, which alter the facts on the ground, pre-empting the final status negotiations, and have negative implications for the Middle East Peace Process" (SC/ 1997/199 Operative Clause 1).

13 The Middle East, including the Palestinian question

17 May 1995—"*Confirms* that the expropriation of land by Israel, the occupying Power, in East Jerusalem is invalid and in violation of relevant Security Council resolutions and provisions of the Fourth Geneva Convention of 12 August 1949" (S/1994/394 Operative Clause 1).

14 The Middle East, including the Palestinian question

31 May 1990—"*Establishes* a Commission consisting of three members of the Security Council, to be dispatched immediately to examine the situation relating to the policies and practices of Israel, the occupying Power, in the Palestinian territory, including Jerusalem, occupied by Israel since 1967" (S/1990/21326 Operative Clause 1).

15 Nicaragua

16 January 1990—"*Expresses* its deep concern over any measure or action that restricts free communication and prevents the functioning of diplomatic missions in Panama in accordance with international law, and calls upon those concerned to take the appropriate steps to avoid the recurrence of such measures or actions" (S/21084 Operative Clause 2).

China

1 Macedonia

25 February 1999—"*Decides* to extend the current mandate of UNPREDEP for a period of six months until 31 August 1999, including to continue by its presence to deter threats and prevent clashes, to monitor the border areas, and to report to the Secretary-General any developments which could pose a threat to the former Yugoslav Republic of Macedonia, including the tasks of monitoring and reporting on illicit arms flows and other activities that are prohibited under resolution 1160 (1998)" (SC/1999/201 Operative Clause 1).

2 Guatemala

10 January 1997—"*Decides*, in accordance with the recommendations contained in the report of the Secretary-General of 17 December 1996, to authorize for a three month period the attachment to MINUGUA of a group of 155 military observers and requisite medical personnel for the purposes of verification of the agreement on the definitive ceasefire, and requests the Secretary-General to notify the Council no later than two weeks before the operation is to begin" (S/1997/18 Operative Clause 1).

Russia

1 Ukraine

26 July 2015—"Decides to establish an international tribunal for the sole purpose of prosecuting persons responsible for crimes connected with the downing of Malaysia Airlines flight MH17 on 17 July 2014 in Donetsk Oblast, Ukraine, and to this end adopts the Statute of the International Criminal Tribunal for Malaysia Airlines Flight MH17 annexed hereto" (S/2015/562 Operative Clause 6).

2 *Bosnia*

8 July 2015—*"Condemns* in the strongest terms the crime of genocide at Srebrenica as established by judgments of the ICTY and ICJ and all other proven war crimes and crimes against humanity committed in the course of the conflict in Bosnia and Herzegovina" (S/2015/508 Operative Clause 2).

3 *Ukraine*

15 March 2015—*"Declares* that this referendum can have no validity, and cannot form the basis for any alteration of the status of Crimea; and calls upon all States, international organizations and specialized agencies not to recognize any alteration of the status of Crimea on the basis of this referendum and to refrain from any action or dealing that might be interpreted as recognizing any such altered status;" (S/2014/189 Operative Clause 5).

4 *Georgia*

14 June 2009—*"Decides* to extend the mandate of the United Nations mission (UNOMIG) for a new period terminating on 30 June 2009" (S/2009/310. Operative Clause 1).

5 *Cyprus*

21 April 2004—*Decides* to terminate the mandate of the United Nations Peacekeeping Force in Cyprus (UNFICYP); *Decides* nonetheless to maintain a United Nations operation in Cyprus which shall be known as the United Nations Settlement Implementation Mission in Cyprus (UNSIMIC)" (S/2004/313 Annex Part A Clauses 1 & 2).

6 *Bosnia*

2 December 1994- *"Reconfirms* that the requirements of all relevant Security Council resolutions, including, in particular, paragraph 12 of resolution 820 (1993) and resolution 943 (1994), shall be strictly applied in respect of all goods crossing the border between the Federal Republic of Yugoslavia (Serbia and Montenegro) and the Republic of Bosnia and Herzegovina, including goods destined for the UNPAs in the Republic of Croatia" (S/1994/1358 Operative Clause—Chapter VII).

7 *Cyprus*

29 April 1993—"*Decides* that, with effect from the next extension of UNFICYP's mandate on or before 15 June 1993 the costs of the Force should be treated as expenses of the Organization under Article 17 (2) of the Charter of the United Nations" (SC/1993/ 25693 Operative Clause 3).

Russia and China

1 *Syria*

22 May 2014—"*Decides* to refer the situation in the Syrian Arab Republic described in paragraph 1 above since March 2011 to the Prosecutor of the International Criminal Court" (S/2014/348 Operative Clause 2).

2 *Syria*

19 July 2014—"*Decides* that, if the Syrian authorities have not fully complied with paragraph 4 above within ten days, then it shall impose immediately measures under Article 41 of the UN Charter" (S/2012/538 Operative Clause 14).

3 *Syria*

4 February 2012—Condemns the continued widespread and gross violations of human rights and fundamental freedoms by the Syrian authorities, such as the use of force against civilians, arbitrary executions, killing and persecution of protestors and members of the media, arbitrary detention, enforced disappearances, interference with access to medical treatment, torture, sexual violence, and ill-treatment, including against children (S/2012/77 Operative Clause 1).

4 *Syria*

4 October 2011—Expresses its intention to review Syria's implementation of this resolution within 30 days and to consider its options, including measures under Article 41 of the Charter of the United Nations (S/2011/612 Operative Clause 11).

5 *Zimbabwe*

11 July 2008—"*Condemns* the Government of Zimbabwe's campaign of violence against the political opposition and the civilian population, which has resulted in scores of deaths, thousands of injuries, and

displacement of thousands of civilians, making it impossible for a free and fair election to occur, and expresses strong concern with the decision of the Government of Zimbabwe to go forward with the 27 June elections" (S/2008/447. Operative Clause 1, Chapter VII).

6 *Myanmar*

12 January 2007—*"Underlining* the need for tangible progress in the overall situation in Myanmar in order to minimize the risks to peace and security in the region," as well as calls for "substantive political dialogue, which would lead to a genuine democratic transition" and calling on the "Government of Myanmar to take concrete steps to allow full freedom of expression, association, and movement by unconditionally releasing Daw Aung San Suu Kyi" (S/2007/14. Last Preamble Clause, Operative Clauses 6 & 7).

Appendix II

1   Africa's goal is to be fully represented in all the decision-making organs of the UN, particularly in the Security Council, which is the principal decision-making organ of the UN in matters relating to international peace and security.

2   Full representation of Africa in the Security Council means:

    i not less than two permanent seats with all the prerogatives and privileges of permanent membership including the right of veto;

    ii five non-permanent seats.

3   In that regard, even though Africa is opposed in principle to the veto, it is of the view that so long as it exists, and as a matter of common justice, it should be made available to all permanent members of the Security Council.

4   The African Union should be responsible for the selection of Africa's representatives in the Security Council.

5   The question of the criteria for the selection of African members of the Security Council should be a matter for the AU to determine, taking into consideration the representative nature and capacity of those chosen.

Select bibliography

David Bosco, *Five to Rule Them All: The UN Security Council and the Making of the Modern World* (New York: Oxford University Press, 2009). David Bosco's highly fascinating history is easily the most enjoyable read on the Security Council.

Ian Hurd, "Myths of Membership: The Politics of Legitimation in UN Security Council Reform," *Global Governance: A Review of Multilateralism and International Organization* 14, no. 2(2008). Ian Hurd is the master of IR legitimacy studies. In this article, Hurd turns his attention to the reform debate, providing one of the strongest rebuttals of enlargement as reform agenda. Hurd's other work is also noteworthy; see Ian Hurd and Bruce Cronin (eds), *The UN Security Council and the Politics of International Authority* (Abingdon: Routledge, 2008) and Ian Hurd, *After Anarchy: Legitimacy and Power in the United Nations Security Council* (Princeton, N.J.: Princeton University Press, 2007).

Sebastian von Einsiedel, David M. Malone, and Bruno Stagno Ugarte, *The UN Security Council in the 21st Century* (New York: Lynne Rienner, 2015). A forthcoming edited volume and successor to *The UN Security Council: from the Cold War to the 21st Century.* The volume features a host of academic analyses and practitioner accounts. It promises to be a important contribution to the literature on the Security Council.

Loraine Sievers and Sam Daws, *The Procedure of the UN Security Council* (4th edition) (Oxford: Oxford University Press, 2014). This is the latest edition of a book that should feature prominently on the bookshelf of every Security Council analyst. At 725 pages, it is simply the most comprehensive guide to the Council.

Edward C. Luck, *UN Security Council: Practice and Promise* (Abingdon: Routledge, 2006). Ed Luck provides a great crash course on the Security Council, and a wonderful point of departure for the present volume (this was the first book I purchased on the council before I embarked on my doctorate). The book is lucid, digestible, and concise – a great overview of the topic.

Sabine Hassler, *Reforming the UN Security Council Membership: The Illusion of Representativeness* (Abingdon: Routledge, 2013). Sabine Hassler's volume is one of the most comprehensive works on Security Council reform. A thoroughly researched and well-argued case, the book covers off the key concepts of the reform conundrum: representativeness, size, power, and inequality.

Thomas G. Weiss, "The illusion of UN Security Council reform," *The Washington Quarterly* 26, no. 4(Autumn 2003)

Thomas G. Weiss and Karen E. Young, "Compromise and Credibility: Security Council Reform?" *Security Dialogue* 36, no. 2 (June 2005)

Edward C. Luck, "How not to reform the United Nations," *Global Governance* 11, no. 4(2005). A brief article published in Global Governance in 2005. Here, Luck summarises the six steps to a cycle of UN reform. He also provides frank assessment of the pitfalls of so-called reform: "adding six new permanent members would put the Security Council on the track to becoming every bit as effective and relevant as ECOSOC."

Index

80–3; reinforcing privilege 5, 80; representativeness 5, 72–80; unanimity and consensus 87–9; winners of reform through expansion 48; *see also* C-10; G4; L-69; new permanency; renewability; UfC; UNSC reform

Fabius, Laurent 111
Fowler, Robert 30–1
France 91; leadership 28 (criticism 29); P-5: 44; Syria 27; UNSC reform 64; veto 110–11, 112
Free Territory of Trieste 12–13
Freeman, Lawrence 127–8

G4 (Group of Four: Japan, Germany, Brazil, and India) 4, 48, 52, 79; African group 79; Asia-Pacific group 79; Brazil 58–9; draft resolution A/59/L.64: 50; E-15: 52; Eastern European group 79; G4 nations preferred model 55; G4 rivals 60; Germany 56–7; GRULAC group 79; India 57–8; Japan 55–6, 69; members and supporters 52, 53; Model A 49; new permanency 52–9; P-11: 2, 44, 52, 74, 86; UNSC reform 48, 50; veto, question of 52, 54; working methods reform 87; *see also* expanded Council; new permanency; UNSC reform
Germany 90–1; G4: 56–7; Libya 57, 91
Gordon, Nora 64, 65–6, 125
Gowan, Richard 64, 65–6, 90, 125
great powers 73, 80; P-5 80
GRULAC (Latin American and the Caribbean Group) 47, 79
Guéhenno, Jean-Marie 38
Gulf War 14, 83, 88

Hammarskjöld, Dag 14, 33
Hampson, Fen O. 29
Hassler, Sabine 85
High Level Panel on Threats, Challenges and Change: Article 23: 89–90; *A More Secure World: Our Shared Responsibility* 48

Hull, Cordell 58
Hurd, Ian 21, 22, 132

ICC (International Criminal Court) 36, 81, 105; *see also* ICT
ICISS (International Commission on Intervention and State Sovereignty) 111
ICT (International Criminal Tribunals) 35–6; ICTFY 16, 36; ICTR 16, 36; *see also* ICC
IGN (Intergovernmental Negotiations on Security Council Reform) 3, 50–2, 125, 130, 134
India 2, 5, 91; calling for enlargement of the council 46; G4: 57–8; India-Pakistan conflict 13, 58, 77; NPT 19, 58; Sino-Indian relations 58; the strongest bid for a permanent seat 57; troop contributor to UN peacekeeping 57, 90
international criminal law 16, 36
interventionism 25, 80, 127, 133; Chapter VII 76; new permanency 59, 74, 134; non-interventionism 59, 76
Iran 58, 108; 1986–1987 Iran-Iraq War 14, 15, 132–3; CBRN weapons 16; sanctions regime 128
Iraq 83, 108; 1986–1987 Iran-Iraq War 14, 15, 132–3; 2003 US invasion of Iraq 32; CBRN weapons 16; sanctions regime 23
Ismail, Razali 47, 67
Israel 19, 23–4, 78
ISS (Institute for Security Studies) 67

Japan 69, 90, 91; G4: 55–6; Japanese Constitution, Article 9: 56; Note 507: 56, 91, 96–8; peacebuilding 56; Sino-Japanese relations 56, 64, 77–8
Johnstone, Ian 21

Kant, Immanuel 6–7
Kilcullen, David 42
Korean War 14, 18
Krauthammer, Charles 26
Krohg, Per 1, 5

Routledge Global Institutions Series

4 The UN General Assembly (2005)
by M. J. Peterson (University of Massachusetts, Amherst)

3 United Nations Global Conferences (2005)
by Michael G. Schechter (Michigan State University)

2 The UN Secretary-General and Secretariat (2005)
by Leon Gordenker (Princeton University)

1 The United Nations and Human Rights (2005)
A guide for a new era
by Julie A. Mertus (American University)

Books currently under contract include:

The Regional Development Banks
Lending with a regional flavor
by Jonathan R. Strand (University of Nevada)

Millennium Development Goals (MDGs)
For a people-centered development agenda?
by Sakiko Fukada-Parr (The New School)

The Bank for International Settlements
The politics of global financial supervision in the age of high finance
by Kevin Ozgercin (SUNY College at Old Westbury)

International Migration
by Khalid Koser (Geneva Centre for Security Policy)

The International Monetary Fund (2nd edition)
Politics of conditional lending
by James Raymond Vreeland (Georgetown University)

The UN Global Compact
by Catia Gregoratti (Lund University)

Institutions for Women's Rights
*by Charlotte Patton (York College, CUNY) and
Carolyn Stephenson (University of Hawaii)*

International Aid
by *Paul Mosley (University of Sheffield)*

Coping with Nuclear Weapons
by *W. Pal Sidhu*

Global Governance and China
The dragon's learning curve
edited by *Scott Kennedy (Indiana University)*

The Politics of Global Economic Surveillance
by *Martin S. Edwards (Seton Hall University)*

Mercy and Mercenaries
Humanitarian agencies and private security companies
by *Peter Hoffman*

Regional Organizations in the Middle East
by *James Worrall (University of Leeds)*

Reforming the UN Development System
The Politics of Incrementalism
by *Silke Weinlich (Duisburg-Essen University)*

The International Criminal Court
The Politics and practice of prosecuting atrocity crimes
by *Martin Mennecke (University of Copenhagen)*

BRICS
by *João Pontes Nogueira (Catholic University, Rio de Janeiro) and
Monica Herz (Catholic University, Rio de Janeiro)*

The European Union (2nd edition)
Clive Archer (Manchester Metropolitan University)

Protecting the Internally Displaced
Rhetoric and reality
Phil Orchard (University of Queensland)

For further information regarding the series, please contact:

Nicola Parkin, Editor, Politics & International Studies
Taylor & Francis
2 Park Square, Milton Park, Abingdon
Oxford OX14 4RN, UK
Nicola.parkin@tandf.co.uk
www.routledge.com

Made in the USA
Middletown, DE
18 September 2020

19986770R00104